Bonaparte in Egypt

HAJI BROWNE (SEATED) AND HIS SERVANT

Bonaparte in Egypt

The French Campaign of 1798–1801
From the Egyptian Perspective

Haji A. Browne

LEONAUR

Bonaparte in Egypt
The French Campaign of 1798-1801 From the Egyptian Perspective
by Haji A. Browne

First published under the title
Bonaparte in Egypt and the Egyptians of Today

Leonaur is an imprint of Oakpast Ltd

Copyright in this form © 2012 Oakpast Ltd

ISBN: 978-0-85706-966-5 (hardcover)
ISBN: 978-0-85706-967-2 (softcover)

http://www.leonaur.com

Publisher's Notes

Contents

Preface   9

The Story of One Hundred Years   11

Links With the Past   19

The Dawn of the New Period   27

A Council of State   36

The Proclamation That Failed   46

A Long March and a Short Battle   55

After the Battle   65

Victors and Vanquished   75

The Gathering of a Storm   87

The Bursting of the Storm   101

After the Storm   116

Peace Without Honour   130

The Siege of Cairo   142

The Price of Peace   154

An Ungrateful People   168

NAPOLEON IN EGYPT

In proportion as we love truth more and victory less, we shall become anxious to know what it is which leads our opponents to think as they do.

Herbert Spencer.

Napoleon's Campaign
in Egypt, 1798.
Scale 1:12 000 000

Miles

MEDITERRANEAN SEA

A   30   B   Long East 33 of Greenw.   C

a

Beirut
Damascus
Tyre
Acre
EnNasirah   Mt.Tabor
Jaffa
Er-Ramleh
Gaza   Hebron   Jerusalem   Dead Sea

Rosetta
Aboukir Bay
Alexandria
Damietta
Mansurah   Ruins of Pelusium
Bahmaniyeh   Segiehpel   El-Arish
Shubra Kheit   Tantu   Es-Salihiyeh
W. Natrun   Zagazig
Kafr Embabeh   Belbeis   Ruins of Heliopolis   Bitter Lake
Gizeh   Cairo   Suez
Pyramids
Fayum
Medinet el-Fayum
Beni-Suef

EGYPT
Arabian
Minieh
Desert
Nile R.
Siut
Girgeh   Keneh   Kosseir

Libyan
L.t Oasis   Bawiti
Desert

S P a l e s t i n e
Jordan R.

Sinai
Peninsula
Akabah
Gulf of Suez   Gulf of Akabah
Monastery of the Mt. Sinai

A R A B I A

RED SEA

Preface

Eight years have passed since I first conceived the idea of writing this book, but it was not until about two years ago that I was able to find time to put together a first rough outline of the form I wished it to take. In the interval I have been obliged from time to time to lay it aside altogether; and, at the most favourable times, have never had more than a few hours a week to devote to it. I had just completed what I had intended to be the last chapter, when events occurred that obliged me to rewrite it, and, that I might do so fitly, await the issue of those events. As the book now stands it is at best but a mere outline. A larger volume than this might easily be written upon each of several of the subjects I have but glanced at, yet I hope I have succeeded in giving a connected and intelligible sketch and one sufficient for the attainment of the chief object I have had in view, that of presenting the Egyptian as he really is to the many who, whether living in Egypt or out of it, have but few and imperfect opportunities of learning to understand him.

For over thirty years I have given of all I have had to give, for the promotion of two objects: first, that Pan-Islamism, which I conceive to be the true interest of the Islamic world; and, secondly, the development of friendly relations between the Moslems of the East and the British Empire. How much, or how little, I have been able to accomplish towards the fulfilment of my aims it is impossible for me to estimate, but from boyhood I have had an earnest faith in the belief that right and truth must in the end prevail, and that he who works for these, or for what he honestly believes these to be, never works in vain.

Knowing the Egyptian as I know him, I cannot but think that he is greatly misunderstood, even by those who are sincerely anxious to befriend him. His faults and his failings are to be found at large in almost any of the scores of books that have of late years been written about him and his country; but, though not a few have given him credit for some of his more salient good points, yet none that I have seen have shown any just appreciation of him as he really is.

Cairo, *May, 1907.*

CHAPTER 1

The Story of One Hundred Years

It was the 23rd of June, 1898. The day in Cairo had been unusually hot and oppressive, but as the sun went down, a cool wind from the north came blowing softly over the city.

I was then living in a little corner of the old town still wholly untouched by the ruthless hand of the "reform" that, in every other part, was busy marring with modern "improvements" the old-time charm of the "City of the Caliphs."

As midnight approached, I went up on the roof to enjoy the cool freshness and quiet of the night, and the stillness was almost unbroken. Now and then in the narrow lanes below, the watchmen, who in their drab-coloured coats and with long staffs and lanterns in their hands, made one think of Old London and the days of Dogberry, called to one another or challenged some belated passer-by, and at times a murmuring echo told of the restless traffic and turbulent life yet stirring in the carriage-crowded streets of the European quarters of the town, but otherwise the silence was undisturbed.

As I stood there, leaning on the parapet of the roof, my thoughts wandered back to the night, just one hundred years before, the 23rd of June, 1798, when possibly some wakeful citizen had stood, perhaps on the very spot on which I was then standing, and gazed upon the very scene, the same limited range of housetops and sidewalls, that was around me. That distant night is one of which the historians of the country make no mention, and yet it is one most worthy of note, as having been at once one of the most peaceful and one of the most memorable Cairo has ever known. Peaceful, for, when not lured from his slumbers by one of the night-quenching festivals he so dearly loves, the Cairene is an early and a sound sleeper, and being then, as now, blessed with an easy-going conscience and unbounded faith in the

11

beneficence of Destiny, we may be certain that on that night he slept the sleep of the just man who is weary. Nor was that night less memorable than peaceful, for little as he could foresee it, it was the last for over a century of time on which the Cairene was to sleep so free from care or thought of the morrow. For, while the city slumbered, away in the villages on the banks of the Nile, sleepers were being unwontedly awakened and dismayed by the sounds of horsemen hurrying through the night with the rushing haste of men who are bearers of tidings of life and death.

Onward, onward they came, these messengers of the night, weary with their long forced ride from Alexandria, the city of the sea, which they had left the day before. Onward, onward as rapidly as they could press forward the steeds that, as one after another failed, were replaced by others seized from the nearest stables "for the service of the State." Onward and onward on their trying ride, spreading as they went the news they bore, news that murdered the sleep of those who heard it, and flung a pall of panic fear over the land.

They were still on the road when the Cairenes rising, as all good Mahomedans should, with the first dawn of day, proceeded to the duties of the morning with the leisurely diligence that is one of their characteristics. But long before midday the messengers had discharged their task, and the fateful news they had brought was being discussed throughout the town. It was news that, to the Cairene, was fraught with most direful possibilities, for it was news that a fleet of English ships of war had arrived at Alexandria, and that the governor of the town, feeling utterly incapable with the scanty resources at his disposal, of offering any effective resistance to a hostile landing, had sent to beg for immediate assistance in men and munitions of war. Many and fervent were the prayers said in the mosques that day, and loud and deep were the anathemas launched against the foreigner who was at their gates. It is not surprising that it should be so, for, of all evils he could imagine, a foreign invasion was, to the Cairene, as to the people of Egypt generally, the one most suggestive of personal loss and misery.

Exactly one hundred years had passed since that day, and the dying hours of that century of time left the Egyptian, as its opening hours had found him, distrustful of the English, rejecting their friendship, and cursing them as foes. That it should have been thus, is one of the problems that perplex those who attempt to know or understand the Egyptian, and as I thought of these things, it seemed to me that living as I then was amongst the most conservative class of the people, the class that still prides itself on living the life its fathers and grandfathers led, and holds all things foreign to be abominations, and yet meeting from day to day with the modern half-Europeanised citizens, and being myself almost an Oriental in thought and sympathy, I could read the story of that one hundred years and comprehend the feelings of the people through all its incidents, better perhaps than any other European, and that by sketching the history of that century as it appears to me, I might help others to understand the people and their history better, and thus aid in promoting the mutual goodwill that is as essential to the interests of the Egyptian himself, as to those of the great army of foreigners who are dwellers in his hospitable land.

As told by the writers of today, (as at time of first publication), the history of Egypt extends over nearly seven thousand years—three score and ten centuries—just one for every year allotted by the Psalmist to man as the period of his life. But of all that great stretch of time the hundred and odd years lying between the fateful 23rd of June in 1798 and the present day, although unfortunately the materials available for a study of it are scant and for the most part unreliable, has more of human interest as a chapter in the history of mankind, than all the long ages that preceded it.

Yet if the reader would rightly comprehend the lesson of this period, he must grasp the fact that in a very full and ample sense all history is a part of one—nay, is but one and the same story writ in different characters. How utterly unlike in all externals are the Gospels written in the Latin, Greek, Arabic, Nagri, or Chinese characters and languages, but the essence and the spirit of all these versions are the same. So it is with the histories of men and nations. The stories of England, France, Spain, India, Egypt, how different! and yet in all that is the final essential of true history—the story of man's combat with his surroundings—the same. It is so because in the last analysis all men are the same, like the ocean, *"His Sea in no showing the same—his Sea and the same 'neath all showing."*

Scattered in the deserts of Persia, the traveller comes upon isolated villages wherein men and women are born, grow up, marry, beget families, and die, and never once pass beyond the mirage-haunted horizon of their little oasis. With world-encircling ideas and ambitions, the traveller thinks of the mad maelstrom of life in the crowded cities of the West, and wonders that men can be so different and still be men, and yet more so, that between himself and these Persians of the

13

desert, drifting through life in a daily round that never changes, never varies, there should be anything in common. And the wonder is, not that they have the same shape and form as he, that they can cry with Shylock, "*If you prick us, do we not bleed? If you poison us, do we not die?*" All that is as nothing, since it lifts the man no higher than the brutes of the field, but in all else, in all that is the essential differentia of man, even in these, these children of the waste are such as we, moved by the same passions, stirred by the same affections, urged by the same desires, however variously all these may find expression.

Further yet afield. The miserable Mahars and Mangs of the Indian Deccan, who, living or dead, are held by all the peoples around them as not less vile than the carrion they do not scorn to eat. Even there among these if you will, you may trace, as the venerable missionary Wilson did, deep buried under the man-debasing foulness of their lives, the humanity of the man as the dominating, all-controlling element, severing them by an immeasurable and impassable distance from the noblest of the animals, and linking them by an inseverable bond to the noblest of their fellow-men. All that may characterise the individual outside of this is but the accident of his life and being; the essential element, guiding and swaying him in all things, is this fundamental, ineradicable humanity.

It is the fashion nowadays to speak of the "Brotherhood of man," but how few realise how absolutely, how completely the phrase expresses the simple truth! a truth that nullifies all the arrogantly-arrayed arguments and fancy-founded fallacies of Haeckel and the whole field of Monists and Materialists. If, then, we would understand the Egyptian or any other people, we must start by recognising that, however wide and apparently unbridgable may be the gulf that divides us from them, whether physical, mental, or moral, it has been caused by the rushing flow of the multitudinous circumstances that have moulded the life and character of each, and, as Mill and Buckle have said, not to any originating difference in our natures.

As a boy at school to me history was the dullest of dull tasks, but when I came to mix with the peoples of foreign lands, and, fascinated by the charm of the living kaleidoscope of Indian life, sought some clue to the myriad-minded moods and manners of its peoples, I longed for a history that should tell me how and why these peoples were so different from, and yet so like, my own. But histories, as they are written, are rarely more than chafing-dish hashes of the "funeral baked meats" of court chronicles served up with a posset of platitudes and pedantry for sauce. From such histories we may gather a great array of useless, and, for the most part, perfectly uncertain and unreliable "facts," but of the true story of a people scarce anything more than a few doubtful indications. For true history is no bald chronicle of events but the history of man's, too often blind but always intuitive, struggle towards happiness. Back in those memory forsaken ages, of which even myth and legend now tell us nothing, men strove in the same ceaseless, never-ending struggle. What if the immediate aim of that struggle varied then and now with time and place? What if the dweller in the ice-cold lands of the North should be ever seeking the warmth from which the sunburnt inhabitant of the torrid zone would fain escape? To neither is the heat or the cold a thing to be desired or shunned save only as either serves to swell the total of his enjoyment of life. But just as the nature of the climate in which they dwell modifies their conception of enjoyment, so also a host of other circumstances, some minute and scarcely traceable in their influence, others broad and plainly visible, mould the ideas and ideals of men and nations.

Thus, and thus only, is it that the Egyptian and the Englishman are so far apart in all that constitutes the individual or national characteristics of each. Thus it is that the restless activity and energy of the one is abhorrent to the other, and that the Englishman today finds the Egyptians, as Herodotus found them so long ago, men "distinguished from the rest of mankind by the singularity of their institutions and their manners." I would, therefore, have my readers avoid the error of judging the Egyptians merely from comparison with their own standards and without due regard to the study of the causes that have made them what they are. If the Egyptian be found lacking in qualities upon the possession of which we justly pride ourselves, he is not for that reason alone to be condemned or despised. He has, even as we have, faults and imperfections that may be justly censured. Like Meredith's Captain de Creye, we are all "variegated with faults."

These but attest our common humanity, and for the Egyptian it may at least be said, that he has that charity that covereth a multitude of sins, the charity of heart that far outvalues the charity of the purse. Judged with equity he compares favourably in many points with many other men. Less backward than the Spaniard, less bigoted than the Portuguese, less fanatical than any other Oriental, not embittered in spirit as the Irish Celts, "patient in tribulation," "long-suffering," placable, forgiving, hospitable; honest and withal one who, like Abou ben

15

Edhem, loves his fellow-men, there is much, very much, in the Egyptian that may well serve to gain him the friendship and goodwill of those who seek to know him as he really is. But with all this there is one difference between the Egyptian and all European peoples that, as it seems to me, forms an almost impassable barrier to the growth of close friendship, or even intimate companionship, between the European and the Egyptian. This difference is in their modes of thinking and reasoning, for not until the Ethiopian changes his skin will the Oriental think or reason as a European does.

There are hundreds of volumes wherein the Egyptian is portrayed as he has been seen or known by the authors, but like all other Easterns, the Egyptian is, and perhaps always will be, something of a mystery to the European. The thoughts and reasonings of the two peoples are so constantly and so utterly at variance on points and matters that seem to each to admit of little or no controversy, that any attempt to reconcile them must be abandoned as impossible. It is a natural result of this incompatibility that the Egyptian as commonly described by Europeans is a very different being to the Egyptian as he really is.

It is so all over the East, through all the widely differing races, nationalities, and religions of the Asiatic continent with, perhaps, the single exception of the Armenians, who in this respect are as distinctly allied to the races of Europe as the Egyptians are to those of Asia. Tourists wander for an hour or two through the bazaars of Egypt or India and flatter themselves that they have seen and can describe the people: young officials tell you glibly that they can read them as a book: the veteran who has grown grey in their service will tell you that the longer he has known them the less is he able to comprehend them.

Orientals generally are capable of a high degree of education or training according to our standards: in India we have men who, in debate and authorship in our language, are entitled to rank with some of our own best men; but mentally even these are apart from us, and in this respect, as Kipling says, "*East is East and West is West, and never the twain shall meet.*" Nor is it we only who cannot understand them, since they stumble as often and err as widely in their efforts to comprehend us, and even, as I think, more grossly and more hopelessly. None the less, it is, I believe, quite possible for a European to at least partly bridge the gulf and become familiar with Eastern thought and sentiment, but to do so he must pay a heavy price, for it is to be done only by one who will give not merely years of time, but years of self-abnegation, of self-suppression, of self-isolation to the task.

Abandoning all that he has been he must seek to become that which he is not, and severing his life from all that has made it his, forego his tastes, stifle his prejudices, ignore his predilections, suppress his emotions, thwart his inclinations, and laughing when he would weep, weep when he would laugh. And with this slaying of his own individuality he must in all things strive to identify himself with those alien to him, ever seeking to see, hear, think, and act as they do. And he must do this not for a week, a month, or a year, but for many years. Not in one city, town or country, but in several, not merely mixing as best he may with the wealthy and the poor, the illiterate and the learned, but learning to be at home in the abodes of the prosperous and the haunts of the miserable, become equally so with the merchant in the bazaar and the wandering *fakir* in the desert. And through it all he must ever be other than his home life and training have made him. Ceaselessly on the alert to detect the nature, feelings, and impulses of others and to hide his own.

And he must be and do all this day and night, in the loneliness of the desert as in the busy haunts of men. And in doing this he is treading a road over which there is no return. The further he goes, the more perfect is his success, the more impossible it becomes for him to regain his starting-point. Never again can he be that which he has been before. He may quit the East, return to the home of his childhood and mix again with his fellows as one of them, but he can never recover the place he has left and lost, for he who goes down into the East, though his heart never cease to yearn for home and the things of home, is daily, slowly, imperceptibly, yet surely, being estranged, and he goes home to find that he no longer has a home, that neither in the East nor in the West, is there any rest for him.

Thenceforth and forever he is alone in the world and, with his own sympathies enlarged and enriched, can hope for no sympathy, no fellowship, amidst all the teeming millions of the earth. Friends and kindred may crowd around his board, ties of love and affection may be renewed, but even with the nearest and dearest the fullness of old-time sympathies can never be revived, for though the East is a bourne from which the traveller may return, it is one from the glamour of which he may never free himself, and as in the East his heart for ever looked yearningly to the West, so from the West it will forever look back with desire to the East. To him the whole world is clothed with the horror with which "*the lonely, terrible streets of London*" so bruised the heart of the Irish poet.

Such is the price that he who would know the East must pay for his knowledge, a price that few have paid, that none would willingly or wittingly pay. "I speak that which I know," for over thirty years have passed away since I first went down into the East, and as "a mere boy," as Lady Burton disdainfully described me, set myself the task I have never abandoned. Consequently, as it is my object in this book to try and show what, as he appears to me, the Egyptian of today is and how he has become that which he is, the picture I shall draw of him will necessarily be unlike those drawn by others, but, although I freely admit that it will be my aim throughout to seek to gain for the Egyptian more generous consideration than he is commonly accorded, my sketch will be as faithful to truth as I can make it: should it fail to be interesting, the fault will assuredly be with the writer and not with the subject.

CHAPTER 2

Links With the Past

To understand the Egyptian as he is, we must go back to that
memorable 23rd of June in 1798, and learn not only what he then
was, but how he had become that which he was. Happily, it needs no
long historical details, or wearisome discussion of remote or doubtful
causes to gain this necessary knowledge. A few words to show how
the Egyptian of today is linked with his ancestors of far distant ages,
and a short sketch of the social and political conditions existing in the
country at the close of the eighteenth century will tell the reader all
he need know to enable him to comprehend the story of the years
that have since elapsed.

Although the people were then well established in the land and
possessed a high degree of civilisation, their history, as we now know
it, dates only from the reign of Menes, somewhere over five thousand
years before the birth of Christ. From that date down to the present
time we have a continuous record, the whole course of which may
be divided into three clearly distinguished periods. Of these the first
was not only by far the longest, but in every way the most brilliant. In
it Egypt was an independent country with a social system of an advanced type, the spontaneous product of the genius of the people, and
it was the one in which, under native rulers, the land was filled with
the marvellous pyramids, temples, and sculptures that, though now in
ruins, still excite the admiration and wonder of the world.

The second period began in 529 B.C. with the conquest of the
country by Cambyses. In it after nearly two hundred years of Persian
rule, interrupted by a brief restoration of the native power, Egypt
was for a little more than three and half centuries in the hands of the
Greeks, from whom in the thirtieth year of the Christian Era it passed
to the Roman Empire. Six centuries later, in 638, when the flood tide

of Islamic conquest first swept westward from Arabia, the country became a prey to the Arabs who, in 1171, were in their turn succeeded by their revolting slaves, under whom as the Mameluk Sultans it remained, until, in 1517, it became a province of the Turkish Empire. In this period, under the sway of foreigners, the country suffered from all the ills we are accustomed to associate with the idea of the dark ages of Europe, and everything that was great or noble in the people or their civilisation perished. It was, indeed, during this time that the world-famous cities of Alexandria and Cairo were built as well as the magnificent mosques that are the pride of all Islam, but these were all the work, not of the people themselves, but of the foreigners by whom they were held in thraldom, and are therefore monuments not of the country's glory but of its shame.

The third and present period began in 1798 when the landing of Bonaparte was the first of the series of events that by the introduction and gradual development of European influence have brought about the now existing social and political condition of the country. In this period Egypt has ceased to be a province of the Turkish Empire, and having acquired the semi-independent position of a tributary State, has been lifted from an appalling condition of social and commercial destitution produced by the ruinous misgovernment and reckless tyranny of a dominant class, to one of unexampled prosperity and of social and political freedom not exceeded in any country of the world.

The three periods into which I have thus divided Egyptian history are then distinguished by differences so deep and so far-reaching that almost the only links by which they can be bound into one consistent whole are the persistence of the people and the preservation of the monuments that testify to their former greatness.

That the Egyptian of today, (as at time of first publication), is in truth the lineal descendant of those who inhabited the country six thousand years ago is beyond all doubt. Wherever we go in the Nile valley or in the Delta we meet with men and women whose faces and features are living reproductions of the portraits of the kings and people of the most ancient times as sculptured by the artists of their days. And in their habits, manners, and customs, we find today striking traces of those that seem to have prevailed when four thousand years before Christ, Ptah-hotep wrote his book of *Instructions*, now believed to be the oldest book in the world. And from their building in those far-off ages down to the present day the pyramids, temples, and tombs have stood surviving witnesses of the early greatness of the country, and, though but heedless spectators of its vicissitudes, silent guardians of its departed glory, ever linking its present with its past.

Closely united as the living Egyptian thus is with his earliest ancestors, all the men and almost all the events that preceded the French invasion are as nothing to the Egypt of today. Not a single ruler, patriot, statesman, demagogue, artist or author, in short, no man or woman that lived before the dawn of the modern period, has been instrumental in the making of Egypt or the Egyptians what they now are. Persians, Greeks, Romans, Arabs, Turks; all these have held the people in bondage, but their influence never reached below the surface of the life of the country, and has vanished completely with the men upon whom it depended, and though some of these have left monuments, all but imperishable, of their greatness and glory, these to the Egyptians, heirs of their creators, are but idle relics of a forgotten and unheeded past.

And as it has been with the men almost so has it been with events, for there are but two of these that, preceding the French invasion, have exercised an influence of such vitality as to survive the great change in the condition of the country that has since been wrought. These two events, with four that belong to the modern period, are indeed all that the whole history of the country presents to us as still clearly and prominently exerting an important and permanent influence upon both the character of the people and the existing circumstances and condition of their country. Of these six events the two that belong to the second period are, the conquest of the land by the Arabs and its subsequent seizure by the Turks. The other four are, the French invasion, the rise of Mahomed Ali, the English occupation and the evacuation of Fachoda by the French.

Each and all of these six events have played important parts in moulding the present-day aspect of Egypt and its people, and the more closely do we study the existing conditions, the more strikingly do these six events stand out from all others as the great and dominating landmarks in the history of modern Egypt. Compared with these all the other incidents of that story of seventy centuries—the long procession of dynasties of *pharaohs, ptolemies, caliphs, sultans, khedives*—are all but shadows that have come and gone. It is not so with the landmarks I have named, for not only are these events that have influenced and are still influencing the thoughts and feelings of the people, but the influence they exert is recognised by the people themselves and must be taken into account in any endeavour either to understand the present condition of the country, or to forecast its future.

Although, therefore, the third of these landmarks forms, as we have already seen, the starting-point of the story of modern Egypt, to rightly comprehend that story it is necessary we should have a clear conception of the effects wrought by the first two events and of the influence these have had and still have upon the affairs of the country.

Let us remember here that Egypt, like most civilised countries, has in reality two stories, one the history of the nation as a political body; in other words, its history as history is commonly understood and written, the record of the rise and fall of its rulers, the tale of their triumph and of their failures, and chronicle of their wars, victories, defeats, and all the events that have made or marred their destinies: the other the story of the people themselves, of the growth of their character and institutions, and of the development of their social and moral surroundings. It is with this latter story that we have to deal, and it is, therefore, from the point of view thus assumed that I have estimated the importance of the events of which I have just spoken.

In the history of some countries the two stories, if rightly told, are so interwoven that they become as one, but in the first and second periods of Egyptian history they have scarce anything in common, for so long as the people remained under the rule of the Pharaohs or of the foreigners who succeeded them they were little more than passive victims of the varying fortunes that affected their rulers, and almost the only fluctuations in their state during the long ages stretching from the time of Menes to the French invasion were those occasioned by the varying degrees of the tyranny to which they were subjected. Now and again under some ruler of more humanity or of greater laxity than others their condition may be said to have for the time improved, but such changes were far too slight and their possible duration always far too uncertain for these benefits to be more to the people than as the grateful but passing pleasure a fleeting morning cloud brings to the traveller in a sunburnt desert.

Hence, such as the *fellaheen* or peasantry were when Cheops was building his pyramid, such they remained in almost all respects down to the arrival of the French. The history of the country has, therefore, in the first two periods little to say of the people. In the modern period the two stories touch each other more closely, for in it the people have begun to have a political existence. They have not, indeed, a representative government, and so they have no direct power, but they have a press, the freedom of which is absolutely unrestricted, and they have a "Legislative Council" as a body of elected representatives, through whom, though they cannot control the action of the government, they are at least able to make their voices heard and their wishes known. More important still, they have begun to comprehend the right of a people to be governed, not only justly, but with a regard to their interests as well as to those of their rulers—a fundamental principle that in the past would have been deemed an unpardonable heresy.

The first step towards the realisation of this improvement, though one for long wholly unproductive of any political benefit to the people, was the Arab conquest, which by the resulting conversion of almost the whole population to the Mahomedan religion, brought about a change still fruitful in its influence upon their ideals and aspirations. To fully describe the importance of this event it would be necessary to enlarge upon the character and tendency of the Mahomedan religion at a length my limits forbid, and I must here therefore content myself with noting that, great as was the moral and mental revolution this conversion occasioned, it was by no means commensurate with that which followed the introduction of Islam into other countries.

On the everyday life of the people it seems indeed to have had but little effect other than that of altering their moral standard and modifying in some slight degree their habits and mode of living. It was, perhaps, inevitable that this should be so, for of all the peoples of the East the Egyptians were, and are, the least susceptible of imbibing the spirit that marked the early spread of Islam, gave it the energy that carried it to victory, and still gives it such vitality as it continues to possess. Christianity had been for a long time the State religion of the country, but it seems clear that the great majority of the people were never more than mere nominal followers of the Cross, and the arrival of the Arabs was, therefore, quickly succeeded by the voluntary adoption of Islam by all but the small minority to whom Christianity was something more than a name and whose descendants constitute the Coptic Church of today.

The political condition of the people was little, if at all, affected by the change in their religion; and consequently, under the Caliphs and their successors, the Egyptian continued to be as he had been before—a man with no higher ambition than that of passing through life with the least possible trouble. From year to year his one prayer was for an abundant Nile and a plentiful crop, not that he might thereby enrich himself, but that he might thereby secure a sufficiency for himself and his family and suffer less from the rapacious tyranny and heartless cruelty of those never-resting oppressors, his rulers and all who, as officials or favourites, were lifted even a little above his own level. It was, and is, of the essence of Islam that it appeals to freemen and favours that love of freedom that is the birthright of every man; but Islam brought no freedom to the Egyptians, save, indeed, the spiritual and moral one their rulers could not rob them of.

So such as he had been before, such he remained after the Arab conquest, but with a loftier sense of the dignity of manhood, a nobler conception of life and of its duties, and a stronger faith in a hereafter that should compensate him for all his sufferings and privations in this life. As an individual, therefore, he was somewhat altered, but as a member of the State—if we may apply that term to one who had no political existence save that involved in yielding to his rulers the utmost pennyworth of value they could wrest from him by tyranny and cruelty—he was the same helpless, hopeless, downtrodden being, less valued and less cared for than the beasts in his fields.

But the conversion of the Egyptians has filled them with that intense attachment to the faith of Islam that, shared by all Mahomedans, has given rise to the charge of fanaticism so commonly brought against them—a charge that, in the case of the Egyptians, if not wholly unjust, is too often exaggerated, although none the less there is nothing excites the wrathful passions of the people or, in milder moods, sways their actions more than their fidelity to their religion. It is the fact that this is so that renders the Arab conquest the first great landmark in the story of modern Egypt, for it is not too much to say that this attachment of the Egyptians to their faith is to the present day the most important factor with which all who are concerned in the administration of the country have to deal.

If socially and otherwise the Egyptians profited but little from the establishment of the *caliphate*, they gained still less from the domination of the Turks. To the people, indeed, this change was scarcely more than a mere nominal one. It left them practically under the same rulers, for though the system of government was modified, it placed the executive power, if not in the hands of the same men as before, at least in those of men of the same stamp, who ruled them as their predecessors had done, in the same manner, through the same agents, and with the same cruelty and wanton oppression. Yet the Turkish, like the Arab, conquest wrought one important effect, the influence of which time has strengthened so that it is only second to that in the urgency of its bearing upon existing conditions. Under the Arabs the Egyptians had been ruled by foreigners, but by foreigners who were in some degree allied to them.

Under the Turks their sovereign was, and is, not only a foreigner, but one of an utterly alien race, wholly separated from them by language, character, habits, by everything, indeed save the bond of their common religion. None the less a spirit of loyalty to the Turkish Empire has grown and spread among the people, which, though it would be an error to credit it with the intensity popular writers of the country ascribe to it, has unquestionably a powerful influence upon the views and opinions of the great majority of the people. To Europeans this loyalty, which, it is worthy of mention here, is shared by the Moslems of India, has always appeared somewhat of an enigma. No one, however, who knows the peoples of the two countries can doubt that, apart from the fact of the *sultan* being the official head of their religion, their loyalty to him is largely due to the desire of peoples who have lost the place they once held in the comity of nations to associate themselves with such kindred peoples as have in some extent maintained their ancient status.

The Indian and the Egyptian Mahomedans alike look back to the time when Islam was the one dominant, unopposable power in their native lands, and, conscious of their own fallen condition, would fain relieve the darkness of their destiny by seeking a place, however humble, within the only radiance they can claim to share. While, therefore, the loyalty of the Egyptians to the Turkish Empire is only a part of their loyalty to their religion, it has this, from the political point of view, important difference—that it is not irrevocable, but more or less dependent upon the *sultan* maintaining his political supremacy in the Mahomedan world, for should he lose the position he holds as the most powerful ruler in Islam, not only the Egyptians, but his own immediate subjects, would feel justified in transferring their allegiance to any ruler who might succeed him.

But absolutely as the *sultan* may depend upon the loyalty of the Egyptians as against any non-Moslem power, yet, as we shall have occasion to see, not only can he not do so as against a Moslem rival, but he can only ensure their loyalty and obedience as his subjects by ceding to conditions they hold they have a right to impose upon him. Were, therefore, the hopes of the large section of the Mahomedans which is filled with the desire for the restoration of an Arab *Caliphate* to be realised it would entirely depend upon circumstances that it is quite impossible to foresee—whether the Egyptians would or would not remain faithful to the empire. Meanwhile the revival of the Arabic power being a possibility too far removed from probability to take a place in the politics of the day, the loyalty of the Egyptians to the Turkish Empire must be accepted as a controlling feature in the affairs of the country.

Such, then, are the links that bind the Egypt of the present day to the Egypt of the past, but important as has been, and is, the part that the Arab and Turkish conquests have played in shaping the present and will yet have in moulding the future of the people, it was not to these events but to others occurring outside the country that we owe the inauguration of the modern period of Egyptian history.

What these events were and how they affected the making of the Egyptian what he now is we have now to see.

CHAPTER 3

The Dawn of the New Period

The period which was to be that of the regeneration of Egypt and its people was ushered in by social and political storm and tempest. But the first warning note of its coming, after a brief moment of panic, was unheeded by the people. Nearly three centuries had passed since the country had been invaded by an enemy. That enemy was now the sovereign power, and under the grasping, selfish rule of its executive the trade and commerce of the country had almost entirely disappeared, and thus isolated from the rest of the world the people had no conception of the growth of the power and civilisation of the European nations. They were, therefore, completely ignorant of the events and political impulses that were, though for the moment indirectly only, shaping the future that lay before them.

There were both Englishmen and Frenchmen in the country at the time, but the rulers of the land, arrogant in their petty might, and the people not less so in their degradation, alike held all foreigners in contempt, and thus profited nothing from their presence. They had, therefore, no means of knowing what the relations between the two great European Powers were, or of anticipating how those relations were liable to affect their country. Yet the fact that brought about the opening of the modern period in their history and thus decreed the ultimate fate of the country was the mutual hostility that swayed the two powers.

This hostility had no relation to Egypt or its people, and, but for contributing causes, could never have affected these, yet it was the desire of the French Government to strike what it fondly hoped would prove a decisive blow at the growth of English power in the East, that was the chief inspiring cause of its decision to order the invasion of Egypt. The Directory, which was at the time the governing body in

France, had indeed more than one reason for taking this step, nor was it under the Directory that the eyes of the French had been turned to the valley of the Nile for the first time. Leibnitz, in 1672, had urged upon Louis XIV. the conquest of the country as an object worthy of his attention, declaring that the possession of it would render France the mistress of the world, and though nothing was done at that time to realise the far-seeing policy he advocated, there can be no doubt that the idea was never abandoned.

Talleyrand, indeed, said that on his accession to office, he had found more than one project for its accomplishment lying in the pigeon-holes of the Foreign Office, and he himself entered heartily into the scheme, believing that it would be a most important move towards the fulfilment of his theory that the future of France depended upon the extension of her influence along the shores of the Mediterranean. Volney, the traveller and author of the *Ruins of Empires*, having visited Egypt had, in 1786, reported that it was in a practically defenceless condition, and Magallon, the French Consul at Alexandria, having for years urged the government to interfere on behalf of its subjects in Egypt, had, in 1796, made a voyage to France with the express purpose of protesting against the indignities and ill-usage from which they were suffering, and fully confirmed the views of Volney and Leibnitz.

The Directory were thus at once shown the possibility of acquiring a colony of the utmost value and provided with a reasonable excuse for its annexation. These and other arguments, against which the fact that the French nation was then at peace and on good terms with the Sultan of Turkey, the sovereign of the country, weighed as nothing, decided the Directory. In March, 1798, therefore, the order to organise an expedition for the conquest of Egypt was given to Bonaparte, and two months later, on May 19th, he set out in command of a vast armada, sailing from Toulon and other ports of the south of France.

Thus it was the aspirations of the French nation for the extension of its influence in the Mediterranean and for the acquisition of new colonies and its conquest rivalry with England, and not events in the country itself, that heralded the dawn of the new period, and eventually, though chiefly indirectly, produced the greatest change in the condition and prospects of the people that their history records.

The rapidity with which the French expedition was prepared, and the secrecy with which its destination was concealed, led the Directory and Bonaparte himself to hope that it would escape all risk of interference on its way to Egypt. In this they were not disappointed, but hearing of the assembling of a great military and naval force in the south of France, and believing that it was intended to make a descent upon the Irish coast with a view to co-operation with the rebels there, Lord Vincent warned Nelson to watch for, and, if possible, destroy it.

The people of India were then, however, like those of Ireland, in negotiation with the French, and in particular the famous Tippoo Sultan, "The Tiger of Mysore," longing to be revenged for the defeat and losses Lord Cornwallis had inflicted upon him, had sought their aid. Nelson was aware of this, and having a strong sense of the danger to English interests in India and the East generally the possession of Egypt by the French would be, guessed the real destination of the expedition, and finding that the French had got away to sea, immediately started in pursuit, and, acting upon his own conception as to its aim, steered straight for Egypt. Bonaparte had, however, after leaving the French coast, proceeded to Malta, which he seized, and being thus delayed some days on his way to Egypt, Nelson passed without falling in with him, and thus it was that on June 21st the Alexandrians were startled by the approach of the English fleet.

As soon as the character of the ships thus unexpectedly appearing on their coast became known the town was thrown into a state of the greatest excitement, and the governor, believing that the fleet was a hostile one, sent off to Cairo the messengers whose arrival there I have already chronicled, and at the same time sent other messengers to summon the Bedouins, or nomad Arabs, inhabiting the neighbouring deserts, to assist in the defence of the town.

Nelson lost no time in sending ashore to seek news of the French, but the reception given to his officers was far from friendly. Refusing to credit the statement that the English came as friends and protectors and not as enemies, the governor openly expressed his distrust, and in doing so simply voiced the feelings of the people. Utterly ignorant of everything outside the narrow range of their own experience, it was indeed impossible for these to comprehend how the occupation of Egypt by the French could be a matter of vital importance to the English. So when Nelson's officers assured the governor that they asked nothing more than to await the arrival of the French and to buy a few supplies of which the fleet was in need, he answered them that they could have nothing. "Egypt," said he, "belongs to the *sultan*, and neither the French nor any other people have anything to do with it, so please go away."

It was a bold speech, and as foolish as it was bold, for no one knew better than the governor himself that he was quite powerless to oppose the English if they wished to land, or to take what they needed by force. It was a speech, too, worth noticing, for it affords a clue to much that puzzles the ordinary critic of Egyptian history. Judged by any known canon of social or international courtesy or policy, it was not less inexcusable than indiscreet, for it was as likely to enrage an enemy as to anger a friend, but it was just what one knowing the people might have expected—the utterance of the impulse of the moment, and, therefore, a full and truthful statement of the speaker's thought. For to the Egyptian mind the visit of a fleet of foreign ships of war could have no other object than the conquest or raiding of the country, hence the English fleet must be a hostile one. It was neither lawful nor wise to give provision or succour of any kind to an enemy, therefore they had nothing to say to the English but "Please go away."

It was thus that the people of Alexandria argued then, and it is thus that the people of Egypt generally still argue. For they have always been incapable of taking a broad or general view of any subject. No matter how many-sided a question may be, they, as a rule, can see but one aspect of it at a time. They look, in fact, at all things through a mental telescope that, bringing one narrow and limited aspect of a subject into bold and clear relief, shuts from their vision all that surrounds it. Hence when, as they can and sometimes do, they change their point of view, the change is commonly as abrupt as it is thorough, and those who see only the surface tax them with fickleness. Of late years there have been signs that, at all events, the educated classes are learning to reason on surer and safer grounds; but if the reader would understand their story, he must ever bear in mind the narrow basis of their judgments and, therefore, of their actions.

While the answer of the governor to the English is thus illustrative of a point to be remembered in the character of the Egyptians, the life-story of the man himself also helps us to more fully grasp their mental attitude under the changing circumstances of the period. This Governor, Sayed Mahomed Kerim, was an Egyptian of humble birth, but one of Arab blood, claiming to be a *Sayed* or *Shereef*, that is to say, a descendant of the Prophet Mahomed's family, and thus one of the Arab nobility. In his early manhood this man, who as a *Sayed*, was and is blessed and prayed for by every Mahomedan in the world at every time of praying, was glad to fill the modest post of a weigher in the customs. Gifted with intelligence and other qualities that commended

30

him to his superiors, by their favour and his own ability he rose rapidly to become the local Director of Customs, and eventually, as we find him, governor of the town. That in this position he had the confidence and respect of his townsmen seems clear; and it is thus evident that, tyrannical and oppressive as was the rule under which they lived, there was an open path to place and power for able men. Bribery and corruption, it is true, were rife, so much so, that we may safely assume that Sayed Mahomed did not attain his high position wholly without their aid, but they did not play the dominating part assigned them by historians of the time.

We shall see but little more of this Sayed Mahomed, for though still a young man, he had but a short span of life to run, yet the little we shall see makes him a notable man, and one that should be studied. Bold, impulsive, proud and fearless, with that decision of character so praised by Foster; quick to decide and unalterable in his decisions, deciding rightly from his own standpoint, but often with too limited a view—emphatically more of an Arab than an Egyptian type, and yet in the few glances we get of him, illustrating, most aptly, the Egyptian character. Thus, as his answer to the English was essentially Egyptian and not Arab in substance and manner, so also was his subsequent action. For an Arab in such a strait would have sought to gain time by fair-speaking, so that he might take such measures as he could, or at the worst secure better terms, whereas Sayed Mahomed spoke in a manner that, had the English been, as he supposed, enemies, must have precipitated hostilities, and having done so, again Egyptian-like, made no adequate attempt to protect the town from the possible consequences of his rashness.

Whether fortunately or otherwise no man can say, Nelson, too intent upon the object he had in view to be moved from his immediate purpose, took the rebuff offered him calmly, and, after a day's rest off the port, sailed away, leaving the Alexandrians to congratulate themselves upon their own astuteness and to indulge themselves in vainglorious anticipations of the prodigies of valour they were to perform should the French land upon their shores.

A week having passed by without the appearance of an enemy, the people had regained their wonted calm, when as unexpectedly as though no warning had been given of its coming the French fleet of twenty-one vessels of war and over three hundred transports was seen in the offing heading for the port. This sudden and unlooked-for proof of the reality of the danger they had refused to credit produced the utmost consternation.

Once more the governor despatched messengers in all haste to the capital, and describing the French fleet as one "without beginning or end," begged earnestly, but all too late, for aid.

The people of Cairo, like those of Alexandria, when their first alarm at the arrival of Nelson's fleet had passed away, seeing in his departure a confirmation of their own conception of his visit, ceased to think of the matter save as the subject of jest, but were overwhelmed with dismay at the new alarm, even the government, which had been but little moved by the first, being now stirred to activity and a sense of danger.

The Government of Egypt was then, at least nominally, such as it had been constituted after the Turkish conquest in 1517 by Sultan Selim. Keenly recognising the impossibility of enforcing his authority in a province of the empire so far off and so difficult of access from his own capital, the *sultan* had, not unwisely, contented himself with organising a system of government that was, in his opinion, the one most likely to ensure the permanency of his sovereignty and guarantee him the receipt of a goodly share of the wealth of his new possession. Egypt was placed, therefore, as the other provinces of the empire then were, and still are, under the government of a *pacha*, who was in effect, though he was accorded neither the style nor the honour of that rank, a viceroy. But the *sultan*, anxious to hold the *pacha* in check by some power ever present and active, divided the territory under his charge into twenty-four districts, and placed each of these, as a kind of local governorship, in the hands of a Mamaluk chief or *bey*.

Of the *beys* chosen for these posts seven were to form a *Dewan*, or Council of State, nominally to advise and assist, but in reality to control the *pacha*, whose decisions this Council was empowered to veto. All real power was therefore vested in the Mamaluks, who, it is perhaps scarcely necessary to recall, were the troops that, originally brought into the country as slaves by the Fatimite *caliphs*, had gradually developed their power and influence until their chiefs had become feudal lords, holding lands and keeping, according to their individual means, troops of mounted followers, whose physical qualities and effective training rendered them one of the finest bodies of cavalry that has ever existed.

As must invariably happen when a weak and incompetent government seeks the aid of slaves or mercenaries to sustain its failing dominion, the Mamaluks had eventually acquired such power that they were enabled to usurp the government of the country, and had, as we have seen, maintained their position as *sultans* of Egypt from the time of Salah ed Deen up to the Turkish conquest. Under the system of government established by the Sultan Selim, though unable to regain the absolute independence they had lost, they soon recovered almost all their former influence and power, and as they controlled the military strength of the country, the small Turkish garrison being quite helpless to oppose them, they soon became, as before, the real rulers of the land.

Being invariably foreigners, or the immediate descendants of foreigners, Circassians, Armenians, or other slaves, it was but natural that these *beys* should have no sympathy for the people of the country, and, with the arrogance characteristic of a military body that has attained political power, despised all outside of their own ranks, and held it a disgrace to intermarry with the Egyptians. Actuated by none but the most selfish aims, they sought and cared for nothing but their own interests, each of them being a veritable Ishmael, looking upon all men as his enemies, only accepting the co-operation of his fellow Mamaluks as a necessary measure of defence, confiding in the loyalty of his immediate followers only so far as he was able to control them by rendering their faithfulness to him conducive to their own interests.

Among themselves they of necessity accepted the domination of the one who by force of arms, intrigues, or other favouring circumstances, was in a position to enforce his will against that of the others, and, as might be expected, the *bey* who held this prominent position was the one to whom the post of Sheikh el Beled, or Governor of Cairo, was accorded, that being the post of all others the most coveted by them, this *bey* being, in practice, the real governor of the country, his power being only limited by the necessity he was under of consulting and conciliating the wishes of the other members of the *Dewan*.

It may seem strange that with the power they thus possessed the Mamaluks should continue to offer even a faint show of respect to the *pacha*, or of loyalty to the empire, for light as was the yoke these laid upon them, it was sufficiently galling to men who lived as they did each wholly absorbed in the prosecution of his own personal aims and interests, and the more so that, as the wealth of the country declined under their greedy and ruthless rule, the remittances of revenue exacted by the *sultan* was a yearly draft that seriously limited their resources.

But if the Mamaluk hated and despised all men not of his own class, he was in turn hated by all others with a hatred all the fiercer and more bitter that it had no outlet. Thus, with no friend upon whom he could rely save his own right arm, the Mamaluk chief, however powerful, was fain to accept the patronage of the *sultan* as the only aid he could look for in his combat with the world, and he must needs, therefore, be content to pay for that aid with a certain tribute of grudging loyalty. Nor must it be forgotten that, ever ready to combine and co-operate against a common foe, each Mamaluk was equally ready to turn his hand and sword against his fellow if thereby he might gain aught for himself. Had it not been for the mutual distrust the knowledge of this fact forced upon them, they might easily have regained the independence wrested from them by the Turks.

This had, indeed, been momentarily accomplished by Ali Bey, who, in 1766, not only succeeded in setting himself up as Sultan of Egypt, but aspiring to extend his rule, had attacked and conquered the Mahomedan holy cities of Mecca and Medina in Arabia. His triumph was, however, but short-lived, for Mahomed Bey, the most trusted of his favourites, to whom he had confided the command of an army for the conquest of Syria, abandoned his task, and revolting, took his master Ali prisoner by a treacherous ambush. Unable alone to maintain the power he had thus for the moment seized, the traitor at once tendered his submission to the *sultan*, and was, in reward for his "fidelity," appointed Pacha of Egypt.

His tenancy of this office was, however, but brief, his death soon after, leaving the country once more a prey to the mutual rivalries of the *beys*. In the contest for supremacy that followed, two of these, freed slaves of his, though constantly opposed to and frequently in arms against each other, eventually agreed to share the power between them, the one, Murad Bey, becoming the military chief of the Mamaluks, and the other, Ibrahim Bey, the Sheikh el Beled.

Under the joint sway of these two men the country enjoyed a brief period of greater quiet and peace than it had known for a long time, and although the tyranny and oppression from which they suffered was little if at all abated, the people had been so completely despoiled before and had so little to lose that, as "He that is down need fear no fall," they had but small anxiety for the morrow.

This was the condition that existed on that memorable night of the 23rd of June in 1798, the eve of the day upon which Cairo had its first warning of the approach of the French. Could a plebiscite of the hopes and fears of the people have been taken on that evening, we may be sure that it would have been unfavourable to any change, and that they would have elected to bear the ills they had, rather than face the possibly far worse any change might bring to them.

CHAPTER 4

A Council of State

As soon as the news of the arrival of the French fleet had been received by Murad Bey, he rode to the country house of Ibrahim Bey, now the Kasr el Aini Hospital, on the east bank of the Nile overlooking the Island of Rhodah.

There a council of the leading men of the city was hastily summoned to consider the steps to be taken for the defence of the country, and it was characteristic of the conditions under which the people were then living, that all those present, with the single exception of Bekir Pacha, the governor and representative of the *sultan's* authority, belonged to one of two classes—the military rulers and the religious leaders of the people. The excitement that prevailed in either class was plainly evident at the meeting, though the feelings and fears induced in each by the news they had met to discuss were very different.

The military element consisted entirely of the Mamaluk Beys, who formed, as we have seen, the real ruling power, their title of *bey*—or, as it is written in the Turkish language from which it is taken, *beg*—being fairly equivalent to that of baron as used in our own country in the days of King John, though it has long since ceased to signify any more than the French Legion of Honour, save that, like our knighthood, it carries a personal title. By the people generally, these *beys* were spoken of as *emirs*, a title properly nearly equal to that of prince, and the one employed by the rulers of Afghanistan, so well known to us as the *ameers* of that country.

I have already spoken of the dominant position the *beys* held, but I may add here, as further illustrating their character, that if they had not, as the French nobles had in the days of Louis IX. and Philip the Fair, the right of carrying on war among themselves, they did not hesitate to put their rivalries to the test of battle. Confident in the prowess of

36

their own body, these men had treated with indifference the alarm occasioned by the arrival of Nelson, but when the warning he had given was confirmed by the presence of the French, and the extent of the fleet that was gathering at Alexandria was known, not only through the exaggerated terms in which Sayed Mahomed had described it, but also by the arrival of reports from Rosetta and Damietta to the same effect, they awoke to the necessity for action.

Centuries had then passed since the Arabs or their Mamaluks had measured their strength against that of European armies, and altogether unacquainted with the advance their ancient foes had made in the art of war, it was perhaps natural enough that they should be a little over-confident in their own might, especially as such stories of the Crusades as still lingered among them were not of a kind to excite any very lively fears of an enemy that, according to these traditions, they had never met but to defeat. Moreover, ignorant as they were of the progress of the world outside their own country, they knew that the Moslem corsairs of the Mediterranean were a constant terror to all ships of Christian countries that had to pass the inhospitable coasts of the Barbary States, and that throughout the north of Africa European Christians were found as the slaves of Moslem masters.

Added to this the fact that the insulting treatment they themselves accorded to European ships visiting their ports, and their tyrannous behaviour to European subjects resident in the country, long continued as these abuses had been, had brought no effective or warlike protest from the nations thus gravely injured and insulted, and we can easily conceive that they placed no high value upon the military or naval power of peoples who thus meekly, as it seemed to them, submitted to such outrages upon their subjects. Hence, while they regarded the present occasion as one calling for active measures of defence, they had no presentiment of the disastrous fate that was so soon to overtake them, and so, undismayed by the news of the arrival of the French, cried vauntingly, "Let them come that we may trample them under our horses' feet!"

As to the second class of those present at the council, the *ulema*, or "learned men," that is to say, those who in virtue of their proficiency in the study of the laws of Islam were the acknowledged and duly graduated religious leaders of the people, these looked upon the danger with very different eyes. Unlike the Mamaluks they were men of the country, allied by blood to its people, and therefore, though like priests and ministers of all religions in all countries, forming a class severed from the great body of the people by special and mutually conflicting ideals, aims, and interests, they were not, and could not be, wholly indifferent to the welfare of the people, of whom, by kinship of every degree, birth, marriage, and parentage, they never ceased to form an integral part.

These, therefore, had a lively fear of the inevitable distress any warlike operations in the country must bring upon the people, while the fact that the enemy approaching was a Christian one, gave to their anticipations a personal character they would not have borne had the invader been of the Moslem faith. Like those of the Mamaluks their conceptions of the character of the European peoples were mainly founded upon the traditions of the Crusades—traditions that included only too many incidents, such as that of the soldiers of the Cross, at the taking of Jerusalem, dashing out the brains of innocent infants; traditions that are still recalled in Moslem lands, and are in no small degree responsible for the anti-Christian and anti-European spirit that exists among Mahomedan peoples.

Their feelings at the thought of the possibility of a French victory were, therefore, quite apart from those of the Mamaluks, if, indeed, these ever gave such an idea a moment's thought. If they did, they still had before them three possibilities—victory, which to them meant gain in many ways; defeat and flight, leaving them at least the hope of retrieving their fortune later on, or in some other land; or death in honourable and glorious warfare, warfare too, that being in defence of Islam, would give them the rank and, better still, the rewards of martyrs for the faith. On their part the *ulema* could see only two possibilities: a victory that, however glorious, would have to be paid for at a heavy cost of suffering to the people, or a defeat involving all that they could imagine of dire disaster and woe.

That we may fully comprehend the influences swaying the members of the two classes of which the Council was composed, we must recall their mutual relations. The Mamaluks, then, being Mahomedans in little more than name, yielding their loyalty to the *sultan* and to Islam simply from a regard to their own interests, were commonly looked upon by the *ulema*, as well as by the people generally, as scarcely better than heretics, while their ceaseless rapacity and heartless cruelty made them at once feared and hated. Conscious of these facts, but not daring to place themselves in open opposition to the *ulema*, they sought in every way to gain these to their support, and more especially by their professions of loyalty to the faith, and by treating the *ulema* with all dignity and respect. This, indeed, they were bound to do, since not only was it in the power of the *ulema* to incite the people against them, but with the aid of the *ulema* of Constantinople to secure the *sultan's* action on their own behalf in case of need. In a word, therefore, while despising the *ulema* with the man of action's contempt for the mere student or scholar, the Mamaluks found it essential to their own safety to cultivate their toleration, knowing well that this was all they could obtain from them.

As to the *ulema*, fully recognising the insincerity of the Mamaluks, they were fain to accept their homage as the only course for them to follow except one of open hostility, which, however little they, as a body, need fear its results, to each one individually involved risks not lightly to be run.

Having no power of excommunication, such as that possessed by the priests of the Catholic Church or the Brahmins, the *ulema* had no direct means of coercing those who displeased them, and were thus not infrequently obliged to accept or adopt a line of conduct that under other circumstances they would have refused to follow. It is, therefore, to their credit that throughout the history of their class, they have always been an independent and, on the whole, a fearless set of men, and that it is but rarely indeed they have been opposed to reason or right as they have understood it, though, unhappily, their conceptions of these have not always been such as enlightened minds could approve. Like the clergy of all churches, with, perhaps, the exception of the Catholic, they have not seldom been compelled to choose between interest and principle. That they should never err in such a case, they must have been more than human.

Diverse as were the interests of the *beys* and those of the *ulema* at this council, the aims and hopes of the two classes were in the most perfect accord, both being dominated by the single desire to concert such measures as should seem best for the protection of the country.

In this they were heartily joined by Bekir Pacha. As the representative of the *sultan's* authority, his chief duty and personal interest lay in seeing that the annual remittances to the *sultan* were made as early and as large as possible, and that the country was kept as free from wars and seditions as might be. So long as he could in some fair measure secure these aims, though always, like all servants of the empire, at the mercy of intriguing aspirants, he might hope to retain, if not his post, at least the *sultan's* favour.

Although thus constrained to court the goodwill of both the *beys* and of the *ulema*, his personal sympathies were strongly with the latter, and were not weakened by his keen sense of the treacherous nature of the friendship for himself and of the loyalty to the Empire professed by the former.

The relations thus existing between the three parties at the council—the one-man party of Bekir Pacha, and those of the Mamaluks and *ulema*—had then been in force for some years, and, coupled with the fact that Ibrahim Bey was a man who, though of approved courage, was withal a constant promoter of peace and concord, had contributed not a little to gain for the people the few years of comparative immunity from care and trouble they had been enjoying.

Murad Bey was a man of different stamp. Of great energy, proud and ambitious, ever ready to sacrifice friends as well as foes for his own profit, he is said to have been at times daring to foolhardiness, and again timid to poltroonery, but always consistently selfish, grasping, and tyrannical. From the time that he and Ibrahim Bey had agreed to work together in the government of the country they had shared between them the greater part of the revenue; and Murad, while constantly adding to his private property large areas of land confiscated from the people under various pretexts, spent large sums of money in developing the military resources at his disposal, constructing cannon, storing ammunition, and building vessels for military service on the Nile.

Passionate, impulsive, and keenly conscious of the fact that the *sultan* looked upon him and his fellow-Mamaluks with no friendly eye, upon hearing of the arrival of the French he jumped to the conclusion that they had come, if not as the allies of the *sultan*, yet with his connivance. For Bekir Pacha, both as an individual and as the *sultan's* representative, he had a contempt that, though veiled under the courtesy of pretended amity, lost no opportunity of wounding his feelings or depreciating his authority. Swayed by these sentiments, he did not hesitate on joining the council to charge the *pacha* with being privy to the invasion, alleging it as inconceivable that the French should venture upon such an undertaking if they had not some reason to look for the support, or at least the countenance of the Turkish Government.

The spirit and tact with which the *pacha* repelled this accusation showed that had he been in a position of greater power he might have proved himself a man better able to deal with the danger they had to meet than was his accuser. It was soon evident, however, that the *pacha* had the confidence of the assembly. Murad was obliged, therefore, to accept his denial, and the attention of those present being turned to the more practical aspects of the subject that had brought them together, after a brief consultation it was arranged that Murad should advance to meet and oppose the French, and, as they all hoped, drive them back into the sea, while Ibrahim Bey was to remain at Cairo and provide for the defence of the capital in the event of the enemy pushing their way so far.

Had the council limited itself to the discussion of these points I might have passed it with briefer notice; but perhaps the only really debatable issue brought before it was one the reception of which throws some light upon the important question of the feelings of those present towards the Christians then living in the country.

Urged, mainly, in all probability, by the desire not to remain a mere silent member of the council, one of those present suggested, as a measure of defence, a massacre of all the Christians in the town. There is, I believe, no record as to who made this wild proposal, but we may be certain that it was one of the youngest, and a man little read in either the history or teaching of his religion.

To the tolerant spirit that now happily prevails in England and the West of Europe, such a suggestion, made, even as it was, in an hour of panic, seems savagely revolting. But in our criticisms of this and other incidents in history we too often overlook the lapse of time and compare the Egyptians and other peoples of the past to that which we are at present, and not to that which we ourselves were at the same time. Thus when we condemn the fanaticism of those who made and supported this proposal at the Kasr El Aini Council, we forget to remember what was even then passing in our own country.

This council was held on the 4th of July, in 1798, and on that day the Irish rebels who had been defeated at Vinegar Hill, on the 21st of June, the very day on which Nelson had reached the Egyptian coast, these rebels were still trembling fugitives sheltering in the mountains and bogs of their native land from the ruthless "no-quarter" pursuit of the vengeance-wrecking soldiers of the Crown. Nor let it be thought that in speaking of this I am taking a partial or party view of the events of those days, for my ancestors were with the pursuers, not with the pursued.

And if it be objected that this was in Ireland, and that the atrocities perpetrated by both parties were due rather to political than to religious rancour, let us go back but eighteen years, for was it not in 1780 that for four days the Gordon rioters held London in their hands, and, crying "Death to the Catholics!" sacked and pillaged, burned and wrecked the churches, shops, and houses of Catholics and of those who favoured the cause of Catholic emancipation? Let it be remembered, too, that the fanatics of Cairo had at least this excuse, that they were in terror of an approaching foe to whom those they proposed to slay were friendly, while the only danger that the London mob had to face was at most a political one, and that one based upon mere possibilities, and not even on probabilities.

Let us—but no! the Reign of Terror in France, the echoes of which were then still ringing throughout Europe, the one unsurpassable horror of all time, that was the maniac outbreak of a people frenzied by the long pent-up wrath of their endless wrongs and sufferings, a horror only possible when the inhumanity of a class had shattered the humanity of the mass. But we may recall the crimes of the commune, which in our own days washed the streets of Paris with blood, and was an unreasoning, insensate outburst of political fanaticism, and also the recent massacres of Jews in Russia.

These events have had but little in common, except that they were alike the products of fanaticism—whether political or religious—but they show that in condemning the fanaticism of the Cairo Council we must make allowance for time, place, and circumstances, and, remembering how much more grievously we ourselves and our European kinsmen have sinned, hesitate to accept such incidents as these as stamping the people as in this respect other than ourselves.

Bearing these facts and dates in mind, let us now learn what was the fate of the bloodthirsty proposal thus brought before the Cairo Council, but first a word as to who and what the Christians were whose lives were thus endangered.

The Christians then resident in Cairo, as in other parts of Egypt, were of two classes, distinguished from each other and from the Mahomedan inhabitants by the different political conditions under which they lived. These classes were the Copts and the Franks. The former were the descendants of those Egyptians who, after the Arab conquest, remained faithful to their religion, and the latter Christians of European origin. The Copts were, and still are, the purest descendants of the early Egyptians left in the country, as since the Arab invasion they have intermarried almost exclusively with their own race, whereas the Mahomedans have freely mixed themselves with the Soudanese and other wholly alien peoples.

Under the Mamaluks the Copts almost entirely monopolised the service of the government as clerks and accountants, and wherever mere clerical skill was an essential. Docile, or rather servile, in their submission to all in authority over them, they were in spirit and act hostile to the people generally, and readily availing themselves of their power as petty officials to further the tyrannous oppression of the rulers, at the same time enriched themselves at the expense of all unable to resist their rapacity. The Franks, who were mostly Levantines, were almost all engaged in trade. Like the Copts they were compelled to live within certain fixed limits of the town, the Frank quarter being the street still known as the Mousky, and now the "Cheapside" of Cairo. This locality was chosen for the accommodation of the European Christians by Salah ed Deen, who, in 1173, granted to the Republic of Pisa the first of the long list of "Capitulations," or Treaties, which the Turkish Government has accorded the European Powers, with a view to encourage their subjects to visit and settle in the country, and which grant to those who do so, special rights and privileges for the protection of their lives and property, and the freedom and encouragement of their trade.

As the Copts then did and still do, the Franks then wore the costume of the country, and at the time of the French invasion, almost all of those who remained at Cairo had been born in Egypt. Earlier in the century there appears to have been a considerable number of foreign-born Europeans residing in the capital, but in 1770, owing to the gross oppression of all foreigners by the Mamaluks, who did not hesitate to despoil them by the imposition of taxes and charges of all kinds whenever the government was in need of funds, the number of French subjects resident at Cairo had fallen so low that there were but fifteen houses there engaged in trade, and a few years later, the French Consul having withdrawn, the number continued to decrease until, in 1785, only three French firms were left, and the English, who had been endeavouring to utilise the desert route between Cairo and Suez to develop trade with India, finding it impossible to contend against the constant raiding of their caravans by the Bedouins and the oppressive exactions of the government, had likewise abandoned the town.

The Christians whose massacre had been demanded at the Kasr el Aini Council were therefore practically all natives of the country, but natives subject to the same vile treatment, gross injustice, and wanton outrage that the Christians of Europe then and even now were, and are, inflicting upon the unhappy descendants of Israel. Indeed, no one who has read the accounts of the recent persecutions of the Jews in

Europe and will compare them with those of Christians in Moslem lands, can fail to admit that the balance to be drawn is in favour of the Moslem.

And there has constantly been, especially in Egypt, this important distinction between Christian and Moslem persecutions, that persecution in Christian lands has almost invariably originated with the people, while in Moslem lands, when not occasioned by the fanatical bigotry of some despotic ruler, it has almost as constantly been the result of a weak and impotent government fomenting fanaticism for the promotion of its own ends. In both cases it is indisputably true that the greater the fanaticism has been, the more clearly and surely can it be traced to the teaching of the spiritual leaders of the peoples concerned. Not that these leaders have necessarily or directly advocated persecution, but that their teaching, even when professedly and honestly denouncing it, has been such that it could have no other effect than that of rendering those who accepted it fanatical in spirit, for of what avail can it be that the ministers of a religion should preach toleration, if at the same time they vehemently denounce the followers of other religions as the "enemies of God," doomed to eternal damnation?

Now let us take note that the suggestion of a massacre of the Christians was made at this council at a moment when almost every possible condition that could favour its acceptance was present, and that in spite of this the proposal was rejected.

There was not a man at that council who did not know that the withdrawal of the protection of the government from the Christians would have been hailed with delight by the populace, not from fanaticism, but for the sake of the plunder that would thus have been brought within their reach. It is, therefore, to the credit of Bekir Pacha and Ibrahim Bey that, waiving the mutual want of sympathy that separated them on ordinary matters, they in this instantly joined in protesting against the suggested massacre. Each of them knew that in thus acting he was risking his own personal interests.

On his part Bekir Pacha was only too well aware that, although he was the accredited governor of the country, the small semblance of authority he was permitted to exercise was accorded to him by the *beys* only for their own purposes; that it was their delight to thwart his aims, tarnish his honour, and diminish his influence on every possible occasion and in every possible way, and that it was to the *ulema* that he had to look for any local support in any contest with his powerful foes.

This knowledge, and the fact that, as we have seen, Murad had openly taxed him with being accessory to the arrival of the French, although his denial had been accepted, might well have caused him to hesitate to speak in defence of the Christians.

None the less he did so, promptly and boldly, and, referring more particularly to the Copts, he reminded those present that as subjects of the *sultan* they paid the Capitation tax, and that while their doing so exempted them from military service, it gave them a right both by the laws of Islam and by the laws and customs of the empire to the fullest protection. Happily for the Christians of Cairo the good counsels of these men, supported by the better informed and more enlightened of the *ulema*, prevailed, and the council, not satisfied with simply deciding the matter thus, issued proclamations prohibiting any interference with the Christians.

This matter having been thus settled, the council broke up never to meet again, and thus the last official act of the *beys* and *ulemas* of Cairo acting together in a Council of State was one for which Christianity and Humanity should never cease to have a grateful memory, the more so that the protection given to the Christians was not limited to mere words, since, finding that the people, whether instigated by fanatics or acting for themselves, were assuming a threatening attitude towards the Franks, Ibrahim Bey had these all brought from the European quarter and placed under the care of his own and other reliable men. For the ladies of the Frankish colony the *bey's* wife opened one of his residences, a palatial building in the southern part of the city known as the Birket el Feel, or Elephant's Pond, then one of the best and pleasantest portions of the town. Thus the safety and decent comfort of the whole community was provided for.

CHAPTER 5

The Proclamation That Failed

As soon as Bonaparte's flagship, *l'Orient*, had arrived sufficiently near to the shore a boat was sent into the harbour to bring off the French Consul, Monsieur Magallon. With their usual want of tact in a sudden emergency the people at once protested against his leaving, and would have prevented his going had it not been that the commander of a Turkish warship then in the harbour, having probably a keen sense of the possible results to himself and his ship a refusal might produce, persuaded the governor to allow him to go. From Monsieur Magallon, therefore, Bonaparte learned the little serious opposition the town could offer, since not only was the garrison limited to a body of about five hundred janissaries, a species of militia possessing scarcely any military training or experience, but it was so wholly unprovided with ammunition and other necessaries that at the most it could make but a momentary resistance.

Bonaparte, influenced no doubt by the fear that Nelson returning might surprise him in the act of disembarking, decided upon landing immediately. It was in vain that Admiral Brueys pleaded for a brief delay, urging that the weather was most unpropitious, and that the roughness of the sea, their distance from the shore, their ignorance of the coast, the rocky and dangerous nature of the landing-place, and the approach of night, all combined to render the operation a most hazardous one. Bonaparte would hear of no delay, and so, the fleet having been warily drawn close to the shore, the task of landing the forty thousand men of the expedition was commenced.

The spot chosen for this purpose was one about three miles to the west of the town, and the first boatloads reached the shore at ten o'clock at night. The beaching of the boats was a work of the utmost danger and difficulty, the darkness upon the rocky beach rendering the scene one of the greatest confusion. Fortunately for the French, no attempt was made to oppose their landing, for had the full resources of the town been brought to bear upon them at this critical point, slight as those resources were, the invaders must have suffered heavily. As it was, Bonaparte himself landed a little after midnight, and having slept for an hour or so upon the sands, set out on foot for the town with a party of four hundred men. He was, we are told, in the best of spirits, and marched gaily along with no ear for the surges beating on the beach, and never recking that, even then, other surges were drearily droning on the shores of St. Helena the melancholy music that was to be the doleful dirge of his dying days.

Just as the day was breaking a number of Bedouin Arabs attacked the little force, but after exchanging a few shots retired beyond range, and Bonaparte, followed near at hand by additional troops, continued his advance without further incident until close under the walls of the town.

Although quite conscious of the hopelessness of their position, the governor and the townspeople determined to resist, and the arrival of the French was therefore saluted with a brisk but ineffectual cannon-ading from the walls. Promptly dividing his force into three divisions, Bonaparte commanded a general assault to be made, and soon, in spite of the fusillading of the enemy and the showers of stones and burning materials thrown upon them, two of the divisions succeeded in scaling the walls, while the third forced its way through one of the gates. A sharp but brief contest followed in the streets of the town, but the governor and the militia having retired to one of the forts, the people, accepting the assurances that Bonaparte had conveyed to them, that he came to re-establish the authority of the *sultan* and to overthrow their oppressors, the Mamaluks, by whom it had been usurped, and that their own lives, property, and religion would be respected, threw down their arms.

The town thus occupied by the French, the governor, short of ammunition, and without hope of succour or aid of any description, yielded to the inevitable and surrendered with his troops. Anxious to conciliate the people as much as possible, Bonaparte at once offered to reinstate the governor upon the condition of his consenting to remain faithful to the French, and the offer having been accepted he was re-placed in charge of the town, but subject to the supervision of General Kleber, who having been wounded in the attack was to remain for the time in command of the French garrison.

Having thus easily established himself upon Egyptian soil, Bonaparte lost no time in preparing for an advance upon Cairo, and the landing of the remainder of the troops, together with the horses for the cavalry, and the whole of the baggage and equipment of the expedition, was pressed forward as rapidly as possible. Both as a measure tending to facilitate this movement and as an important part of the policy he had resolved to follow in his dealings with the people, Bonaparte set himself to gain their friendship. Strict orders were, therefore, issued that the people were not to be molested in any way, and some soldiers having been detected in looting after the surrender of the town, he seized the opportunity to give a proof that his assurances were not intended to be an idle parade of words, and had the offenders summarily and severely punished. In this, as in other ways, it is evident that Bonaparte was under the impression that he could gain, if not the full allegiance, at least the passive neutrality of the Alexandrians, and, indeed, it was clear from the preparations that he had made prior to his actual arrival in the country, that he had looked forward to being received by the Egyptians as a deliverer and saviour.

Two of these preparations deserve special mention here. One, curiously characteristic of the French spirit of the day, was the provision of an immense number of tricoloured cockades to be distributed to, and worn by, the people as evidence of their reconciliation with the French; the other was the composition and printing of a proclamation in Arabic which was to serve at once as a declaration of the aims and intentions of the French in entering Egypt and as an appeal to the friendship and support of the people. This proclamation has, with great justice, been described as a most extraordinary document. Of considerable length, it was framed throughout with the object of soothing the religious susceptibilities of the Egyptians, and was so worded as to represent Bonaparte and the French, if not as Mahomedans, at least as the special friends and protectors of Islam. Beginning with the well-known formula,

"In the name of the most merciful God," invariably prefixed by Mahomedans to all important writings, it proceeded to state that the French had arrived in Egypt with the intention of punishing the Mamaluks for their ill-treatment of the French and other foreign subjects resident in the country; to restore to the people themselves the rights of which they were deprived by their tyrannical rulers, and to re-establish the authority of the Sultan of Turkey, the legitimate sovereign. Had the proclamation stopped here it would in all probability have been accepted by the people as a genuine expression of the purport and scope of the invasion, but it went on with great elaboration to promise boons to the people that these were quite incapable of either comprehending, or had they done so, of appreciating. These promises were couched in the spirit then dominant in Paris, and, indeed, throughout France, that is to say, the spirit of the Revolution, the "Gospel" of "Liberty, equality, and fraternity," that was to turn the world into a paradise.

Thenceforth, it declared, it was to be possible for all to arrive at the most exalted posts; public affairs were to be directed by the most learned, virtuous, and intelligent; and thus the people were to be made happy. All this was in perfect accord with the theory and teaching of the Mahomedan religion, but it was in some respects very far indeed from the practice to which the people had for centuries been accustomed. As to the promise of opening out facilities for advancement, we have seen that in the governor of the town the people had a convincing proof that these already existed, and it is not at all probable that it ever occurred to them that the facilities at which the French general hinted were of a very different nature to those of which Sayed Mahomed had availed himself. It is not surprising, therefore, that these promises seemed to the Egyptians nothing more than mere idle bombast, and were by them promptly put down as simply a valueless bid for their favour.

What followed was still less calculated to win their confidence, for, as evidence of the friendly spirit of the invasion, Bonaparte went on to declare his faith in the unity of God, his respect for the Prophet Mahomed and the *Koran*, and to claim that he had "destroyed the Pope" and the Knights of Malta because they were the enemies of Islam. Such professions as these to the Egyptians carried on their face their own contradiction, for, if Bonaparte was in truth a Moslem, or a friend of Islam, how was it, they asked, that he had entered the dominions of the *sultan* without some acknowledgment from him of the claim thus made to be acting upon his behalf?

The concluding phrases of the proclamation came, too, rather as an anti-climax to the lofty spirit of benevolence and high aim that the body of it was intended to express, for the whole rigmarole—I can scarcely find a better word for it—came to an end with a commonplace promise that those who submitted to the French should be "exalted," while those who opposed them should be "utterly destroyed." One can fancy how the Egyptians smiled to themselves at this conclusion and accepted it as in itself the whole object and purport of the document. But whatever may have been their private feelings on the subject, and their own historians have told us how little reliance they put upon the professions and promises thus offered them, it is certain that outwardly the Alexandrians discreetly accepted both the cockades and the proclamation without any show of feeling other than that of amused curiosity.

So little, indeed, did they betray their true feelings, the French were unquestionably deceived, and did not realise how different these were from those which they had expected the proclamation to excite. But it is certain that none of the Egyptians were in the least deceived by its plausible tone, and while they refrained from any display of hostility to the French, they were looking forward with high hopes to their early annihilation by the Mamaluks.

Large numbers of this proclamation having been printed by the aid of the Oriental type and printing presses, with which the expedition was provided, Bonaparte not only had it freely distributed in Alexandria, but forwarded copies of it to Cairo and elsewhere, using as his messengers for this purpose some Mahomedans he had released from the prisons of Malta, and had brought with him to Egypt, with the object of utilising them as interpreters, and in the hope that gratitude for their release would cause them to espouse and advocate his cause.

That Bonaparte's conception of the probable attitude of the Egyptians towards the expedition was entirely erroneous, is clearly evident from the whole tone of the proclamation. Thoroughly well-informed as he appears to have been, as to the actual state of the country and the deplorable misgovernment from which it was suffering, he and his countrymen seem to have jumped to the conclusion that they would be received and welcomed by the people as deliverers. That they should have so thought is a very noticeable fact, for it plainly proves that all the information that they had received, including that furnished by the Consul Magallon and other French residents, afforded no ground for any suspicion that the French would incur any risk or danger from fanaticism on the part of the people.

That they were keenly awake to the absolute necessity of conciliating the intense attachment of the Egyptians to their faith, is not more clearly evident than is the fact that they had no conception of hostile fanaticism as a factor to be considered in their relations with the people. It was with self-satisfied bigotry and not fanaticism that Bonaparte considered he had to deal, and as we shall see in the course of our story, he was so far perfectly correct. But in arguing from this assumption, he was led by ignorance of the facts with which he had to deal, to absolutely erroneous conclusions. The fundamental error into which he fell is one that, notwithstanding the warning his experience might have conveyed, was repeated by ourselves in the beginning of the present occupation of the country, and distinguishes even the recommendations of the brilliant statesman, Lord Dufferin.

This error was the assumption that a people so sorely oppressed and downtrodden as were the Egyptians could not fail to be grateful and friendly to anyone who should deliver them from their oppressors, yet it needed but a slight acquaintance with the people, with the evils from which they suffered, and the light in which they regarded those evils, to show that this could not be so. As we have seen, the dominant trait of the Egyptians' character was, and is, their loyalty to Islam, and, as a consequence, their fidelity to the *sultan*. Knowing nothing of the Christian religion or of the political condition of Christendom, they looked with contempt upon Christians generally as in every way their inferiors, and recalling how great but unavailing had been the struggle of the Christians for the possession of the Holy Land, they regarded their long abstention from all further effort for its conquest, as a proof and tacit admission of their inability to face the armies of the *sultan*.

Thus the Egyptians of that day, as indeed the great mass of them still do, believed the *sultan* to be the greatest and most powerful monarch in the world. That his rule in Egypt was little more than nominal they did not perceive. In their eyes it was a real and substantial power. That they should thus be blind to what seems to us self-evident truth, is largely to be attributed to the fact that almost all that was done in the country, was done in the name of the *sultan*. It was in his name and, as they were often assured, by his authority that the taxes and exactions by which they were ruined were imposed; and since *beys*, *ulema*, and all who represented these, were never tired of preaching that all resistance or disobedience was rebellion against the *sultan*, it was but natural that they should regard his rule as very far indeed from being the mere fiction it in reality was.

Nor did the tyranny and oppression from which they suffered in the least militate against their loyalty, for they never for a moment attributed their woes or troubles to any more distant cause than the officials by whose immediate action they were inflicted. That the higher officials did not protect them was, as they thought, due solely to the misrepresentations, indifference, or ill-faith of those through whom alone they had access to them. There was not a fellah in the land in those days, nor is there one today, that did not or does not believe that if he could only lay his grievances before the *sultan* or the *khedive* in person, he would receive perfect justice and ample compensation for all his tribulations.

They were confirmed in this opinion by the nature of the oppression from which they suffered, for this necessarily varied in different places and at different times, according to the personal character of the officials through or by whom it was inflicted. Moreover, among the worst of their tyrants of high degree, however callous these might be to the miseries of the people, there were but few, indeed, who did not consider it a matter of policy, and therefore in some measure one of pleasure, to pose now and then as a minister of justice, or as a benevolent benefactor. To render justice to the poor and oppressed, and to be profuse in liberality, have ever been the surest means of gaming the real and sincere approbation or devotion of the Egyptians, as of all other Oriental peoples.

None knew this fact or appreciated it more thoroughly than some of those from whose heartless cruelty they suffered most. Nor was it difficult in the roughly organised administration of the country, for the worst of their oppressors to play the part of an innocent victim of the wrong-doing of others, for when appealed to, the higher officials threw the blame upon their subordinates, while these in their turn professed to be the unwilling but helpless agents of their superiors. Thus finding all complaints useless, the sufferers always nourished the thought that if they could only plead their case personally to the *sultan*, the one and only person who could not urge his own impotency to remedy the evils they complained of, or grant them the relief they sought, they would be assured of the justice and mercy they so sorely needed, and which they could gain from no other.

That this should be their idea is not surprising, for they have never as yet risen beyond the idea of personal government, and therefore while their belief in the immaculate justice and merciful disposition of the *sultan* was liberally fed and encouraged by all around them, even by those from whose tyranny and greed they suffered most, they attributed his evident indifference to their griefs to the impossibility of his knowing and dealing with all the acts of all the officials of his empire. Of an organised system of government, in which the controlling power is able to exert itself through all grades of its officials from the highest downwards to the lowest, they had no knowledge, and indeed could have no conception, nor even in the present day, after more than twenty years' experience of the working of such a government, have they any just idea of its organisation or of the principles or methods upon which its efficiency is based.

Nor did the Egyptians see the cruelty and tyranny from which they suffered from the same point of view as the French did, or as we do. However limited and imperfect were the services that the government rendered them, they were conscious that they were in some respects dependent upon it. It at least afforded them a certain amount of protection for life and property, and gave them a rude system of justice. As a return for these benefits they admitted its right to tax them, and being thus entitled to tax them, it naturally, as it seemed to them, taxed them to the uttermost penny, while they as naturally paid as little as possible.

It was simply a contest between the government and the governing, not unlike the bargaining that was their sole method of carrying on trade in the bazaars and markets, and they had and could have no conception of any other manner in which the government of a country could be conducted. It was not possible, therefore, for the people to grasp the ideas Bonaparte was anxious to press upon them, nor was it possible that during his short stay in Alexandria they should have any opportunity of gaining a better comprehension of his Republican ideals, so utterly at conflict with all their conceptions of the relations of a people with those who governed them.

It is true, that having confirmed Mahomed Kerim as governor of the town, Bonaparte had appointed a *Dewan*, or council of seven members, to aid in the administration of its affairs; and to these he, no doubt, gave sage advice and strict injunctions as to the duty of governing for the benefit of the people; but while to him this council was suggestive of the Directory of Paris, and thus of the spirit of the Republic, to the Alexandrians it was but a reproduction of the *dewan* at Cairo, which to them was typical of nothing but tyranny and torture. Further, the strict discipline necessarily enforced upon all the members of the expedition, and rendered all the more evident and striking, in that all ranks were ceaselessly engaged in the work of receiving the stores from the ships and preparing for the advance, when contrasted with the laxity that prevailed in the ranks of the Mamaluks and of all other troops that the people had previously had any knowledge of, was not at all calculated to point with any but sarcastic emphasis the doctrines of equality and fraternity presented to them.

And not only the spirit, but even the wording of the proclamation, was fatal to its success. In it Bonaparte had declared that "all men are equal in the sight of God." This, to Mahomedan ears, was nothing short of rank and absolute blasphemy, for the *Koran*, which to the Mahomedan is the veritable and literal "Word of God," emphatically asserts, and in the plainest terms, the contrary. This clause was, therefore, in itself sufficient to stamp the whole document with impotency, and showed how imperfectly Bonaparte and his advisers were informed on some of the points most affecting the sentiments and spirit of the people.

To the Moslem all mankind is divided into two classes—the Moslems and the non-Moslems. Between these they admit of no equality whatever. Among themselves they are theoretically equal. As a Moslem the *sultan* himself is no more than his meanest servant. Hence the democratic spirit that exists everywhere in Islam, and hence the freedom with which servants and even slaves address their masters. But in contradiction to this, the man who rules, whether as *sultan* or as his deputy, or in any minor degree as the master of a household or otherwise, is, from the mere fact of his ruling, regarded as being invested with a Divine right to do so, since, although one subject to limitations, it is equally a doctrine of the *Koran*, that all power is from God, and therefore to be respected as such.

Thus in Islam democracy and despotism go hand in hand; and while the Moslem of Egypt, as the Moslem of other lands, sees no incongruity or difficulty in this, to the European mind the concurrent operation of these two conflicting theories gives rise to many puzzling problems. Yet the solution is simple enough, for the democracy of Islam is the democracy of the grave, the recognition of the truth that all must die, and that in death all are equal; for though this belief be shared by all men as the one great truism of life, among Mahomedans everywhere there is an active sense of its verity that ever present with them modifies all their views of life and death in a manner wholly foreign to the European mind.

To the Egyptians, therefore, the proclamation was a mere flood of futile folly, and so little confidence was placed in its promises or in the French protestations of amity, that many of the people who could afford to do so made haste to quit the town and seek shelter in Rosetta or elsewhere, wherever they could speed by boat or by land as opportunity offered.

CHAPTER 6

A Long March and a Short Battle

That the advance to Cairo might be made as rapidly as possible, Bonaparte decided that the bulk of his army should proceed direct to Damanhour, a town thirty-three miles to the south of Alexandria, and on the most direct road to the capital. As it would have been most difficult to convey the heavy baggage of the expedition by this route, lying as it did across desert and inhospitable lands, General Dugua was commissioned to proceed by the longer but more practical and agreeable one, usually adopted by the people of the country. This led by Rosetta, a town situated four miles from the sea on the west bank of the Nile, and forty-five miles from Alexandria. Thence as soon as the town had been effectively occupied the general, accompanied by a flotilla of boats, which were to be sent round from Alexandria as transports for the troops and stores, was to proceed up the Nile to Ramanieh, where his division was to meet the main army under the immediate command of Bonaparte.

Short as was the distance to Damanhour, the march over the barren, burning desert was a most trying one for the troops of the expedition, who suffered severely from the want of food and water. Meat and bread were alike unobtainable, and the famished soldiers at the end of their day's march had to satisfy their hunger with rude cakes of grain crushed between stones and roughly baked on open fires. Nor did their arrival at Damanhour bring them any very sensible relief or encouragement, for there, as everywhere on their advance, the plain evidence the miserable homes of the people afforded of the chronic poverty in which they lived, was such as to wholly damp the ardour of the troops and fill them with dismay at the prospect of a sojourn and campaign in such an inhospitable country.

Fortunately for them it was the season of the water-melons, and on these and the coarse cakes of bread I have mentioned they had to support the fatigues of their march as best they might. To add to their distress, small parties of Arabs hovered perpetually around the wretched column and, while keeping at a safe distance from the main body, lost no opportunity of slaughtering every weary straggler who got separated from his companions.

These Arabs were all Bedouins, or nomadic Arabs belonging to tribes inhabiting the deserts that skirt the Delta and valley of the Nile, and, possessing all the characteristics of their race, were nothing more than restless, roving bands of robbers, ever ready to prey upon all unhappy enough to fall into their hands. Arabs by race and Mahomedans by religion, they yet acknowledged no ties of kinship or brotherhood outside of their own tribes, and were as ready to plunder, ill-use, and massacre the Egyptians as the French, or to unite with either against the other as the interest of the moment might dictate. In attacking the French, therefore, they were actuated by no other desire than that of securing the spoil of arms and other loot to be reaped from the bodies of their victims.

Of the people of the country the French during their advance saw almost nothing; for fearing, not only the loss of everything they possessed, but that they themselves might be seized and compelled to work as slaves in the service of the army or be sent for sale in foreign lands, and dreading that their women would be outraged and their children massacred, they had, at the first warning of the approach of the French enemy, hastened to forsake their homes and seek safety in distant towns or villages, taking with them their flocks and herds and as much as possible of their portable property.

After spending a couple of nights at Damanhour in taking the rest it so badly needed, the army set out for Ramanieh by a route leading almost at right angles to that which they had been following. On the way they fell in with a small party of the Mamaluks, with which they had a brief skirmish, Bonaparte himself narrowly escaping capture while separated, with a few attendants, from the main column of the force. At Ramanieh the army again halted for a rest and to await the arrival of the division for Rosetta.

Meanwhile General Dugua, with the force under his command, had arrived at Rosetta. This town, now fallen into decay and yearly decreasing in population, was then a place of considerable importance, owing to its position at the mouth of the Nile, and the fact of its being the chosen terminus of the journey by boat of those travelling between Cairo and Alexandria. In many ways one of the most pleasant spots in the whole of Egypt, surrounded by gardens and cultivation, and having markets well filled with all the produce of the country, it was at that time probably of all the towns of Egypt the one most attractive to foreigners.

Here as in other parts of the country there was a small colony of Christians, including some few Europeans, and when the fugitives from Alexandria began to arrive with the news of the landing of the French and their occupation of that town, these were thrown into a state of the greatest alarm by the prompt outbreak of a fanatical cry for their assassination. There were in the town a number of Candiotes who had been drawn to it by the fact that the acting governor was a countryman of theirs, and these had brought with them the fanatical spirit common in their own country. It was among these that the demand for a massacre of the Christians was started, and the governor himself appears to have been favourable to the project, which was in fact one of plunder rather than of murder, conceived in the hope that it would provide the Candiotes with an opportunity of enriching themselves safe from all danger of retribution.

That the Egyptians did not readily accept the proposal is clear, as otherwise it would undoubtedly have been put into immediate practice. Happily for the Christians the opposition offered was strong enough to delay the carrying out of the plan the turbulent bigots had formed. The matter was still being heatedly discussed when messengers arrived from Alexandria with copies of Bonaparte's proclamation. These testified that so far the people of that town had not only received generous treatment from the French, but were being liberally paid for all that the French required from them.

The assurances they thus received that they had nothing to fear as to the safety of their lives or property were accepted by the people of Rosetta with the thoughtless impulsiveness of the true Egyptian. From a condition of panic and despair they passed at a bound to one of scarcely doubting satisfaction. Difficult as it may be for us to realise it, this was but the natural consequence of the character of the people and of the circumstances in which they lived. As we have seen, their rulers, the Mamaluks, were foreigners, to whom they were united by no ties, whom they hated and feared, and from whom they could expect no benefit or advantage of any kind.

When, therefore, they learned upon the testimony of their own countrymen the generous behaviour of the French to their vanquished enemy, they had reason rather to welcome than to oppose them, their hostility to the idea of being ruled by Christians being for the moment wholly outweighed by the rapture of their release from appalling alarm.

The panic that had arisen being thus allayed the counsels of the tolerant Egyptians were promptly accepted, and so heartily was the suggestion of an attack upon the Christians repudiated by the people in general, that the governor and some others who had been foremost in the agitation for the massacre hastened to leave the town, and set out to join the forces of the Mamaluks. As soon as their departure became known it was decided to offer no opposition to the French, and when, therefore, General Dugua approached he was met by a deputation which presented the keys of the town to him, and gave him an assurance of the peaceful disposition of the inhabitants.

Of the attitude of the people of Alexandria and Rosetta towards the French after their first glad acceptance of the terms accorded them, we can learn little from the native historians; it is not, however, difficult to conceive what that attitude really was. Assured for the time of the peaceful possession of their lives and property, and freed from the terrors that had assailed them at the first coming of the enemy, they were in no mood to criticise or question the good faith of the newcomers, but as their feelings regained their wonted calm doubts began to arise. It was to them an altogether unheard-of thing that a military force should occupy a country and not at once seize upon its wealth, or at least exact tribute of some kind or other from the people.

Nor could they forget that the Mamaluks when moving in the country, alike in time of peace or in time of war, ruthlessly took all they needed as a right to which they were entitled. How came it, then, that the French not only did not despoil them, but paid and paid well for what they required? Why should they pay when they could if they would help themselves freely? That, in the abstract, it was but justice the people knew well enough, but that any people could possess so keen a sense of justice as to thus conciliate its claims they could not understand, for, after all, they could not but regard it as a voluntary foregoing of what seemed to them a clearly defined and evident right.

Hence they were not long in coming to the conclusion that the forbearance of the French might be a mere trick to enable them to more effectually carry out some deep-laid scheme for the complete spoliation of the people. But the honest man has an inborn sense of the false and true that is seldom misled. Rogues batten upon rogues. And the Egyptian, by nature honest in thought and deed, is not slow to recognise honesty in others, so the straightforward sincerity of the French beat back his doubts; and baffled and perplexed he took refuge in a halting attitude, a kind of moral armed neutrality, neither fully accepting nor yet rejecting their proffered friendship. As to the French, though they could not but be conscious that they had not been received with the open arms they had expected to greet them, and were sensible that the people were acting under some restraint, they had no just conception of the real position, and believed that only a little time was needed to enable them to gain the full confidence of the people.

On the whole, therefore, things went smoothly enough in the early days of the occupation, and General Dugua lost no time in establishing at Rosetta a provisional administration on the lines of that set up by Bonaparte in Alexandria. This having been done the work of preparing a flotilla for the ascent of the Nile was carried on with the utmost despatch. It took but a few days to do all that was necessary, and General Dugua, leaving a small force as a garrison, started with the division under his command for Ramanieh, which he reached without encountering any difficulty or opposition.

From Ramanieh the French army continued its advance upon Cairo, and keeping always within touch of the west bank of the Nile, was accompanied by the flotilla laden with the stores and provisions. As is usual at that time of the year, the ascent of the river was facilitated by the strong winds which blow across the country and up the river with a strength more than sufficient to counteract the swift downward flow of the stream. Coming from the north these winds naturally tend to moderate the temperature, but though thus beneficial to the troops, who had already suffered so much from the parching heat of the desert, they proved an unexpected source of danger, for, its progress exceeding that of the troops, the flotilla unexpectedly encountered near Shebriss a fleet of gunboats from Cairo that, borne by the downward current of the river, was approaching it at a speed not less than its own, and was supported on either bank of the river by large bodies of the Mamaluks.

The French finding themselves thus running right into the midst of their enemies, while their own troops were as yet too far behind to succour them, the boats of the flotilla were hastily anchored in the positions they happened to occupy at the moment. A brisk engagement followed, in which the invaders were so sorely pressed that had not the explosion of a powder magazine on one of the Egyptian boats suddenly thrown the enemy into confusion, it is more than probable the whole flotilla would have fallen into the hands of the Egyptians. As it was, several of the French boats were captured, and their crews either driven into the river or ruthlessly cut down, and their decapitated heads exposed to the horrified gaze of their companions.

So evident was the danger that pressed them that Bertillon, one of the *savants* who accompanied the force, began to fill his pockets with stones gathered from the ballast of the boat in which he happened to be, and when asked why he did so replied that he might sink rapidly rather than fall into the hands of the enemy. Fortunately for the French, ere the Egyptians had recovered from the confusion the explosion had created the fall of night put an end to the contest.

Meanwhile, intelligence of what was happening having been sent to Bonaparte, he had hastened to the aid of the flotilla, but only succeeded in reaching it too late to take any part in the battle. Early the next morning, however, the two armies were drawn up in battle array, and the Mamaluks, with the fearless and impetuous bravery which had always been characteristic of them, lost no time in opening the attack and charged right up to the French line. Their accustomed dash and reckless courage proved, however, of no avail, and they were speedily repulsed by the veterans to whom they were opposed, who kept their ranks unbroken, and waited for the near approach of their foes to pour upon them a galling and destructive fire.

Baffled by the stolid calmness of the French, and puzzled by the impotency of their own wild charge, the Mamaluks hastily withdrew beyond the French line of fire and halted, apparently uncertain what course to pursue. In the pause that followed an incident occurred curiously illustrating the widely different ideas and spirit by which the two armies were animated. One of the Mamaluk Beys rode unaccompanied towards the French line, and boldly challenged his foes to single combat; but, for the French at all events, as a French historian cynically remarks, the time for such chivalrous exploits was past, and to the disgrace of the French the daring Mamaluk was shot down on the spot. Discomfited by the repulse they had sustained and with the whole of their forces thrown into disorder, the Mamaluk chiefs decided to abandon the field, and turning their horses' heads retreated precipitately towards Cairo.

Thenceforth the expedition continued its advance without further opposition until within sight of Cairo, always keeping close to the river, not only for the sake of the water, but for that of the more abundant supplies obtainable in its vicinity, and for the mutual support of the army and the flotilla. To carry out these latter objects more effectually a strong detachment was sent across the river to guard the east bank, and to forage in the villages of the Delta. On both sides of the river the troops continued to be harassed by small parties of the Bedouins, who, following all their movements, availed themselves of every opportunity of cutting off stragglers.

One of these raiding parties having surprised a junior officer, whom from his uniform and appearance they mistakenly supposed to be a man of high rank, carried him into their camp with a view to holding him for ransom. Bonaparte at once sent a messenger to offer a few guineas for his release. Thereupon a dispute arose among his captors as to which of them should receive the ransom, and was continued so heatedly that the chief of the party, enraged at their obstinacy, declaring that none of them should have it, shot the unfortunate prisoner and sent the ransom back.

As the force moved onwards towards Cairo the heat became daily more and more oppressive and enervating to the troops, to whom, fresh from the genial spring climate of Southern Europe, the fierce and dazzling glare of the sun in the shelterless lands through which their route lay, was little short of an agonising misery. To add to their sufferings the food obtainable was, as before, neither adequate nor adapted to their needs.

It was not until the 20th of July that the army caught its first sight of the pyramids and of the Mokattam hills overhanging the city of Cairo. As they had drawn nearer the capital, the evidence of a greatly increased density of population, and the greater abundance and variety of the supplies they had been able to secure, gave the jaded troops fresh energy and hope. They were still much more than a long day's march from the pyramids when Bonaparte received intelligence that the Mamaluk army was encamped at Embabeh, a village on the west bank of the river, at the spot where it is now crossed by the railway bridge. As it was then evening the army was halted and bivouacked for the night at the hamlet of Om el Dinar, but only to rise and resume its march before the first dawn of day.

Animated by the prospect of the combat now but a few hours before them, and which, as they confidently expected, was to gain them a fair reward for all the hardships they had been enduring, the troops pressed onward eager for battle, but it was not until two o'clock in the afternoon that at the end of a twelve hours' march, they found themselves in touch with the enemy.

Learning that the Mamaluks had entrenched themselves in front of the village of Embabeh, and had planted a battery of forty guns in position behind their trenches, Bonaparte decided that it would be necessary to advance in such a way as to be able to attack the enemy's position upon its flanks, and he therefore so disposed his forces that, each division marching in the form of a hollow square, the whole would approach the enemy's position in the form of a crescent, and so that, while the right and left wings would threaten the Mamaluks' flanks, the centre would be prepared to repulse the front attack he expected them to make according to their custom.

Murad Bey, who, with his long white beard covering his breast, was in personal command of the Mamaluks, was not slow to detect the aim of the French general, and quickly ordered Eyoub Bey, one of the best and bravest of the Mamaluk commanders, to advance and attack the division of General Desaix, who was moving round towards the west with a view to outflanking the left wing of the Egyptian position. Eyoub, who had under him a large and fearless, but wholly undisciplined, body of cavalry, at once bore straight down on the French without seeking cover of any kind, and, when within charging distance, dashed upon the French square with the wild cries, brandishing of arms, and tumultuous crowding customary to all Oriental warfare of that day.

Faithful to the orders they had received, the French withheld their fire until the enemy were close upon them, so close that the ruthless rending of the ranks of the Mamaluks by the fierce hail of shot poured upon them was all insufficient to stay their headlong charge, which, bearing down the resistance of their foes, carried them into the centre of the broken square. But the French veterans, always cool and prompt, turned about, and the Mamaluks, finding themselves encircled by their enemies' fire, fought their way back and out of the square, but only to bring themselves under a heavy crossfire from the square and the division of General Kleber, who was moving up to its support. Eyoub's party being thus routed, the French made a direct attack in force upon the entrenched position in front of the village of Embabeh and carried it at the bayonet's point, while the divisions forming the left wing of the attack pushed on between the village and the river.

The Mamaluks were thus caught between the horns of a crescent that was threatening to close and entirely surround them. Seeing the danger, Murad Bey at once withdrew his men, and sought the scanty shelter of a grove of date-trees at a little distance from the village. In doing this he was compelled to leave behind him some hundreds of the Mamaluk troops who, caught between the French and the river, utterly unable to defend themselves or to fly, were deliberately shot down by the French or perished in an attempt to escape across the river.

As one historian says, it was no longer a fight but a massacre; and thus ingloriously ended what is termed by the Egyptians the "Battle of Embabeh," and by the French the "Battle of the Pyramids," a battle by which the power of the Mamaluks was shattered, and Bonaparte was left for the moment master of Egypt; a battle in which the steady discipline of modern warfare proved once and for all its immeasurable superiority over the wild chivalry of the past; a battle which, apart from this and the vast consequences that have resulted from its issue, is scarcely worthy of remembrance.

The whole combat had lasted rather less than an hour, and when it was over the French soldiers, forgetting their fatigues and weariness, turned the field into a vast mart, bartering and selling the spoils of rich armour, weapons, apparel and other things they were able to reap from the bodies of their vanquished foes.

Murad Bey, finding it impossible to recover his position, and that his forces were too disorganised and dismayed by a system of warfare so strange and incomprehensible to them to make any further effort, abandoned the field and hastened away to his summer palace at Ghizeh, whence, after collecting his most portable valuables, he set out for Upper Egypt.

The justice that never fails hàd thus overtaken the iniquities of the Mamaluks. For centuries they had desolated the land, sacrificing all else to their own ambitious greed, and now they were "shattered and broken," never again to recover. For a short time they were to struggle and hope vainly for a return to power, but it was not to be. The fiat of Heaven itself was against them, and the decree of their doom went forth as infinitely more inexorable than the laws of the Medes and the Persians as Omnipotence is to impotency. Some years afterwards, when the British were encamped upon the banks of the Nile near Beni Souif, a poor, half-blind, wholly-destitute fugitive sought protection and a pittance at their hands.

It was Ibrahim, the last of the great Mamaluk *beys*, a man by no means typical of the baser of his class, with many faults, yet with some good points, one who under happier circumstances might have left an honourable record of service for the welfare of his fellow-men. As it was, his fate was but a part of the answer of that wrath that had at last heard the cry of the distressed, and avenged the wrongs of the widow and the orphan.

CHAPTER 7

After the Battle

Before leaving Cairo to meet and oppose the French advance, Murad Bey had arranged that a large chain was to be stretched, as a boom, across the river, and batteries erected upon the adjacent shore to play upon the enemy in the confusion he anticipated would arise from their meeting with this obstacle. It was not, however, until the news of the defeat of the Mamaluks at Shebriss had thrown the capital into the utmost confusion, that any serious efforts were made to prepare the defences of the city. When that news came to the people, who had been looking forward to receiving tidings of the destruction of the French, then Ibrahim Bey and Bekir Pacha, filled with alarm at this first note of disaster, jointly called upon the whole population to take up arms and hasten to the riverside for the defence of their homes and families.

Weapons and ammunition were served out as long as they could be got to all comers, and when the supply of deadlier arms ran short, the deficiency was made good in intention, if not in fact, by the distribution of *naboots*, long staffs of hard wood, which the Egyptians of the lower classes are accustomed to use much as our distant forebears used their quarter-staffs. Other impromptu weapons were provided by the people themselves, such as knives lashed to the end of long sticks, this primitive arm which could be either wielded as a lance or thrown as a javelin being destined at a later date to deprive the French of one of their ablest generals.

Cairo was at that time separated from the river by an open stretch of ground, now covered by the avenues lined by the villas and mansions that form the Kasr el Aini and Ismailia quarters of the town. At the north end of this space was the small town of Boulac, which served as the port of the city then as it still does. This was the spot chosen by Ibrahim Bey as the headquarters for the defence of the town, and here and around the people were gathered, and quantities of stores and ammunition of every kind collected, whatever was needed or desired, if not found in the magazines of the State, being seized without ceremony wherever it could be got.

For several days the space between the two towns was covered with the crowds coming and going, engaged in the transport of the various materials required; and so great was the haste to finish the work and the desire to help it on, that men of almost all degrees assisted in the task. As it was impossible to find accommodation for everybody at Boulac, a large number of the people returned to their homes in the city to pass the night and gain well-earned repose, but only to return at the first dawn of day.

Unwonted and severe as was the labour they had to undergo, all worked not only willingly but with the greatest enthusiasm, and with all the needless noise and tumult that is a never-failing part of any exertion the Egyptian worker is called upon to make. Not unnaturally the workers encouraged each other by vaunting cries of contempt and derision for the enemy they were expecting, and thus incurred the censure of the Egyptian historian Gabarty, who condemns such conduct as lacking in the dignity that should distinguish the defence of Islam.

The *ulema*, who, like the Druids of old, have always been exempt from military service and taxation, were like them, not backward in encouraging others in their toil or in assisting in such ways and manners as befitted their character. Very properly they busied themselves especially in prayer, and at all the stated hours of worship offered up fervent supplications to the Deity for protection and victory, and, the children of all the schools being under their charge, they gathered these and led them in processions reciting invocations suited to the occasion.

The *dervishes*, or, as they are often incorrectly termed, the "Monks of Islam," who are in reality simply members of lay confraternities, such as those of the Catholic Church, also assembled themselves and paraded the streets flying their banners and accompanied by the weird Arab music of pipes and drums that, unwelcome to European ears, has a strange fascination for the Arab and Egyptian, and, like the "*Ça ira*" or "*Marseillaise*" in the streets of Paris, fills its hearers with a fierce longing for action and excitement, a wild craving to be up and doing they know not what, or why.

Some of the wealthier citizens left the town to seek refuge in the neighbouring villages, others simply sent their families and valuables away and joined the gathering at Boulac, and the town being thus practically deserted—even the Sheikhs el Harah, petty officials appointed in all the quarters of the town to look after public order, being engaged at Boulac—the streets, which in ordinary times were swept and watered daily, were neglected, and business of every kind being of necessity at a standstill, the poorer classes, who lived from hand to mouth on their daily earnings, no longer finding any employment, were driven by sheer starvation to seek in robbery and crime a means of living.

The *dewan* having been broken up by the departure of Murad Bey and others of the Mamaluk chiefs, no regular council could be held; but Bekir Pacha, with some of the *ulema* and leading men who remained, held frequent consultations and were in constant communication with Ibrahim Bey, who remained at Boulac day and night to supervise the work there and along the river, by the side of which batteries were being erected for a distance of nearly three miles north of Boulac.

Ibrahim Bey appears to the last to have preserved his confidence in the certainty of the Mamaluks proving victorious, but Bekir Pacha, when the news of the near approach of the French was received, decided in conjunction with some of the *ulema* to make an attempt to treat with the enemy. With this object in view they sent for a Monsieur Bandeuf, who was regarded as the leader of the French colony, and begged him to tell them candidly what he thought was the object of the invasion. He, of course, was no better informed upon this point than they were themselves, but he could at least form an idea, and his reply was that he believed it most likely the French desired nothing more than a free passage through the country to enable them to proceed to India to join their countrymen there in their struggle with the English.

Accepting this as, at least, a possibly true explanation of the invasion, they proposed to Monsieur Bandeuf that he should go as an envoy from them to Bonaparte, and assure him of their willingness to facilitate him in every way if such were his object. Not without some hesitation occasioned by his fear that it would not be possible for him to reach the French camp in safety, Monsieur Bandeuf consented to do this, and was preparing to set out, with an escort of the Mamaluks of Ibrahim Bey for his protection, when the reverberations of the cannon at Embabeh were heard, and they realised that it was too late for such an embassy as they had proposed.

As soon as Ibrahim Bey heard the commencement of the battle he began to take such steps as he could to forward assistance to Murad Bey, but long before any effective move in that direction could be made the battle was over, and Ibrahim Bey, hearing of the flight of Murad, hastened back to Cairo with Bekir Pacha, to take their families and valuables and flee.

Words fail to describe the panic that overwhelmed the people. Utterly helpless, and unaccustomed to think or act for themselves, unarmed and without any possible means of defence, they saw themselves, deserted by their leaders, at the mercy of a foe from whom, as they thought, they could expect no quarter and no pity, while the military force, in the protection of which they had felt such unbounded confidence, was in full flight leaving them to their fate. To any unwarlike and helpless people to be thus suddenly abandoned as a prey to an unknown foe must have seemed an appalling disaster, but in this case no circumstance seems to have been wanting that could by any possibility add to the natural terror of the people at the calamity that had so suddenly befallen them. In less than an hour they were plunged from an exulting ecstasy of triumphant anticipation to the crushing despondency of the direst despair.

The consternation that had been occasioned by the first news of the defeat of the Mamaluks at Shebriss had been largely, if not wholly, dissipated by the representations of the Mamaluks, and so loud and blatant were the vauntings of the people that Gabarty, whose Arab blood had but little sympathy for any open expression of the emotions, speaks in the most contemptuous terms of their conduct as wholly unworthy of a people deserving of any esteem. Nor had the Mamaluks, knowing well how little love the people bore them, neglected to contribute all they could to their fear of the French by attributing to these the lust of rapine and bloodthirsty cruelty. And with the news of the defeat and flight of Murad Bey came the tale of the slaughter of the Mamaluks by the riverside to confirm and augment the worst fears of the people.

Later on reports were spread that the French were still busy slaying and destroying all before them, and, Ibrahim Bey having ordered the burning of all the boats to prevent the French using them to cross the river, the people, ignorant of this, took the dense columns of smoke arising from the riverside as confirmation of the ruthless ravage the

French were said to be wrecking. In the dire madness of the despair that seized them no room was left for any other thoughts than those of self-preservation, and, as the evening closed in and night fell, the whole population, laden with all they could carry of their goods or wealth, streamed out of the city gates. In the maddened rush for safety, all the claims of blood and friendship were forgotten, and men and women alike, frantic from their fears, fought their way through the fleeing crowds heedless of parents, wives, brothers, sisters.

More than one writer has taken this wild exodus as a text to accuse the people of cowardice. Nothing could be more unjust. They were flying from what to them was a very real and immediate danger, and for the most part on foot from mounted foes. They could see no other choice but fly or die, and the darkness of the night, the suddenness of the danger, everything helped to urge them onward. Not more sure was Christian that he was fleeing from the City of Destruction than were they. It was a panic such as seizes a people with all the more uncontrollable force in that it comes as a sudden revulsion from peaceful ease; one such as those that in our own days in London, Paris, New York, and San Francisco have turned laughing, joyous crowds of pleasure-seekers into mobs of frenzied fugitives.

When in the days of the dynamite scare in London the crash of the Scotland Yard explosion was heard in the Strand, men dashed here and there for safety from the danger that had passed. Not long after I saw a roomful of men hurl themselves headlong down a narrow flight of stairs, fleeing madly from the report of a detonating cigar! I have seen panic seize a thousand emigrants on board a German ship in mid-ocean; another, the pilgrims for Mecca on an Austrian ship in Bombay Harbour; another, the *coolies* working on the Hurnai Railway in Beloochistan. In these cases the panic-creating danger was an imaginary one, and yet in real danger these same victims of panic remained calm and collected. It was so, as we shall have occasion to see, with the unhappy Cairenes.

I have spoken already of the fears that the coming of the French had awakened in the hearts of the people, and to the Cairenes it must have seemed on that most miserable of nights as if the realisation of all the worst of those fears was but the question of a few moments. As the evening had fallen had they not seen the columns of flame-emblazoned smoke that to them were a proof of the ferocious fury of the foe? Had they not seen the Mamaluk chiefs, the bravest of the brave, fleeing for life with breathless haste? With no arms, no leaders,

69

nothing but instant flight as the only means of safety they could conceive, surely a people who had not been panic-stricken in such dire peril would have been a nation of heroes such as the world has never yet seen!

But if safety for them lay outside the city, it was not beneath its walls, for there the Bedouin tribesmen, whom Ibrahim Bey had summoned to assist him in the defence of the town, disappointed of the plunder of the French army to which they had looked forward as their only inducement to take part in the contest, with untroubled consciences turned to the pillage of the unhappy fugitives as a heaven-sent compensation for their unrealised hopes. Nor were they content with the rich plunder that thus easily fell into their hands, but with wanton savagery murdered the men and outraged and slew the women. Thus finding at the hands of their co-religionists, who had been summoned for their defence, no better mercy than the unrestrained cruelty they feared from the French, the unhappy people, or at least so many of them as escaped from the Bedouins, returned to their homes, while the Mamaluk chiefs and their followers rode away through the desert indifferent to the fate of all they had left behind them.

Meanwhile the French army, after a short rest, had advanced along the left bank of the river as far as Ghizeh, a village lying in the line between the city and the pyramids, where Bonaparte decided to encamp. On their way from Embabeh the troops had an opportunity of seeing across the river the town of Cairo and the nearly mile-wide stretch of open land lying between, studded with the gardens and summer residences of some of the wealthier of the *beys*. Elated by their victory, and perhaps still more so by the rich loot they had gleaned from the dead bodies of their fallen foes, they forgot the fatigues of their long advance, and set themselves to enjoy the rest they so much needed and the comparatively luxurious fare they expected to compensate them for all the hardships they had endured. Many were the castles that rose in the air as they sat around the bivouac fires, and joked and jested until, wearied by the labours of the day, "*Nature's soft nurse*" lulled them to the repose she withheld from their vanquished enemies.

But the coming of daylight on the morrow of the battle brought to the horror-whelmed citizens some small gleam of comfort. Fugitives from the west bank of the river told them how the French had settled peacefully down at Ghizeh, and people coming into the town from Boulac explained the fires that had added so much to the terror of the night. With the calmer mood thus induced came the remembrance of what they had heard of the mildness and humanity of the French at Alexandria and Rosetta, and along the line of their advance, and though the mourners were wailing for their dead and missing in every street and corner of the town, and their homes had been dismantled or disordered by the flight of the night before, and swept by the thieves of the city of whatever had been left behind, the people still, as ever, impulsive and hopeful, began with the truest of courage to repair as best they might the havoc that awful night had wrought, and to face the fears and dangers yet before them with a spirit little short of heroism.

Early in the morning the *ulema* and the few leading men who remained in the town gathered together to consult as to what course it would be best for them to follow. They had not much scope for discussion, for they recognised from the first that the only question left for them to deal with was how best to conciliate the conquerors. Eventually it was agreed to send a deputation to the French camp to announce their submission and crave the forbearance and protection of the French general, and thus to ascertain as far as possible what they had to hope and what to fear. Tactless as he is in a moment of emergency, when he stays to take thought with himself in calm and serious mood, the Egyptian not unfrequently shows a wisdom that his critics seldom accord him.

Thus, wholly inexperienced as they were in such diplomatic matters, they wisely judged that to send as the representatives of the town men who could claim to be neutrals would tend to further the objects of their mission. Two Maghribeen Sheikhs—that is members of the *ulema* from the Barbary States—were therefore selected, and with many injunctions and entreaties counselled to plead the cause of the town in the most earnest manner they could achieve. Accompanied by the prayers and blessings of the whole population, the deputation, not without some small lingering doubt as to the nature of the reception that might await it, set out for Guizeh.

Bonaparte, to whom their coming was not so unexpected as they themselves thought it to be, received them with the affability he so well knew how to show, and which throughout his stay in Egypt did much to lessen the friction between the two peoples. One of the *sheikhs* was able to speak French, and had had some experience of French manners, and he, acting as spokesman, discharged his task well and discreetly, and concluded his address by an appeal for clemency. Bonaparte replied that he was the friend of the Egyptians—not

71

their enemy—that he came to the country to release them from the tyranny of the Mamaluks, and in short gave them a verbal restatement of the proclamation, with many fine flourishes, about the high aims and noble ideals by which the French were actuated. So with many fair words the deputation was dismissed, but with the request that the chief men remaining in the town should wait in person upon the general to hear from him the arrangements he proposed to make.

All the town was awaiting the return of the deputation with an eagerness and suppressed excitement that made their short absence seem an age, and great was the relief when they were seen once more approaching the landing, and great the joy with which the news they bore was received throughout the town. No time was lost in responding to Bonaparte's invitation, and, taking with them the keys of the city, all the chief men set out for Guizeh, anxious at once to gain renewed assurance of the fair hopes awakened by the report of the deputation, and at the same time give the French general a proof of their readiness to comply with his desires.

Bonaparte was, if possible, more gracious than before, and again dilated upon the purely friendly and beneficent intentions of the invasion, of his sympathy for Islam, and his desire to make his coming the opening of a new era in the history of the people, who were thenceforth to enjoy all the blessings that the establishment of the Republic had already conferred upon the French themselves. He was listened to with the emotionless stolidity of the Oriental, but not without occasional exclamations of approval, yet as he went on his hearers were moved by steadily growing wonder at and distrust of a speech so utterly unlike anything they had ever heard of, or conceived as possible, from the lips of a conqueror.

They had, indeed, read the proclamation, copies of which had been sent to Cairo, but it had failed with them, as with the people of Alexandria, to convey any intelligible conception of the ideas it was intended to impart, and the "Little Corporal's" discourse reaching them through the mouth of an interpreter helped them nothing at all to grasp the real aims and object of the French. All that they could comprehend was that they were expected to accept the French as their rulers; that their lives, property, and religion would be respected; and that the French were as eager to reward their friends as to annihilate their enemies. But loyalty to the French and loyalty to the *sultan* were so mixed up in the proclamation and in Bonaparte's speech, and were in themselves, in the eyes of the Egyptians, two such absolutely

72

irreconcilable things, that the *sheikhs* were completely bewildered by the attempt to solve the enigma thus presented to them. So they were content for the moment to accept the French assurance that they were to be treated as friends, and for the rest God was great, and they put their trust in Him.

But if the speech of Bonaparte thus made upon them but little impression of a definite kind, the courtesy shown them by all the French with whom they came in contact was not so barren. Accustomed as they were to the hollow insincerity of court life under the *beys*, the *sheikhs* could not fail to appreciate the genuine character of the politeness with which they had been received by the French. It was due rather to this appreciation than to the plausible promises of the general that they returned to the city somewhat, though not wholly, reassured as to the immediate future. On their part the French were sufficiently pleased with the docility of the deputation, and from the dignity, self-possession, and courtesy of its members augured well for the realisation of their own views.

As a consequence of the good understanding thus arrived at, boats were sent over to Guizeh to convey the advance guard of the army to Cairo, and returning after sunset with a detachment of the troops escorted through the town by some of the leading men, and, lighted by torches, led to the citadel, of which it took possession.

The following day the bulk of the army was moved across the river, and historians record, with some disgust, the revolting glee with which the soldiers fished out of the stream the hideously swollen and disfigured bodies of the Mamaluks and of the horses that had perished in the attempted escape from Embabeh that they might despoil the miserable carcases of whatever remained upon them of value. We must remember, however, that in those days the armies of Europe were recruited from classes that had scarcely as yet been touched by the advance of civilisation. Nowhere was human life then regarded with the sanctity a more enlightened age accords it. To his superiors the soldier was of no value but as "food for powder," and it is not surprising that the little value placed upon his life by others should lead him to look upon the lives of his foes at a still lower rate and deprive him of all feelings of humanity towards them.

As to the people of the town, released from the fears that had plunged them in such disastrous despair and as responsive as always to the impulse of the moment and the play of their surroundings, these received the French, if not with the open arms that Bonaparte had

73

looked for, at least with a toleration and absence of hostile demonstration that speedily put the French at their ease. Everything thus bidding fair for the realisation of all his hopes, Bonaparte himself crossed over the river on the 27th of July and took up his quarters in a new palace that Elfy Bey, one of the wealthiest of the Mamaluk chiefs, had only just had completed and furnished in a magnificent manner, on the bank of the small lake to the north-west of the city, the site of which is now occupied by the garden and buildings of the Esbekieh quarter of the new town.

CHAPTER 8

Victors and Vanquished

Bonaparte having thus accomplished the first and, though he did
not think so, last step on the way towards the building of the great
Eastern Empire that he had dreamed was to "take Europe in reverse,"
despatched a portion of the army in pursuit of the fugitive Mamaluks,
and settled down in his new quarters to scheme and prepare for the
future.

The troops remaining in Cairo, in the best of humour at the agreeable change the city gave them from the hardships of the advance,
began with the rough good-humour of the soldier to fraternise with
the people. At first, diffident and distrustful of the French, the lower
classes seeing that these went about unarmed, and that not only were
their own lives and property respected, but that even the common soldiers paid liberally and promptly for all they needed, were not slow in
adapting themselves to the position. They were still depressed by the
loss of kin and property that had resulted from the panic, but believing, as all Moslems do, in Pope's doctrine that "Whatever is, is right,"
they rapidly recovered their wonted cheerfulness, and wherever the
French went in the town they, like *rasselas, "met gaiety and kindness, and
heard the song of joy or the laugh of the careless,"* almost untinged by the
dread of reflection Imlac so dolefully attributed to the merriest.

That the people should have thus readily accepted the rule of an
alien army has often enough been the subject of cynical criticism on
the part of authors compiling the history of the country from such
documents as fell in their way, but from their ignorance of the people and of humanity in general, incapable of reading aright the true
meaning of the records they perused. Let us avoid their error, and
try to grasp the real meaning of this oft-condemned "levity" of the
Egyptians, and let us do so with the more seriousness of purpose that,

in learning what we can of the real attitude of the people towards the French in 1798, we shall be learning much that will help us to understand their attitude towards the English in more recent years.

To begin with let us note that in fraternising with the French the Cairenes were true to their natural instinct, for they are and always have been a volatile, light-hearted people, fond of jest and pleasure, enjoying the present with no heed for the morrow, and the rank and file of the invaders being of the same temperament, these traits supplied a ready bond of good feeling between the two bodies. And in yielding to the spirit of fellowship thus engendered the Egyptians betrayed no trust, and were guilty of no treachery or disloyalty. To the Mamaluks they owed no more loyalty than did the Saxon English or the Celtic Irish to the Normans, and no more love than the French revolutionists had had for the aristocrats.

Whatever of loyalty they had was given to the *sultan*, and since Bonaparte professed to respect his authority and to be acting in his interest, this loyalty was not outraged by the presence of the French. Nor did the flight of Bekir Pacha, the *sultan's* representative, impeach the good faith of the French, for it was no uncommon sight to see a Turkish governor in arms against, or fleeing from, his sovereign.

Two things only separated the victors from the vanquished, the want of a common language and the religion, or rather irreligion, of the French. The former was too trivial a matter to sway either the French or the Egyptians, and the latter, though it was an effectual barrier to any deep friendship between the two peoples, was scarcely any restraint upon such purely social intercourse as was possible between them. Finally, the Egyptians had but one of two courses open to them—they must either frankly accept friendly relations or offer a sullen and unavailing opposition. This was so because they were as little anxious for, as incapable of, self-government, or self-protection. Without some governing body to direct the affairs of the country they would have been like a flock without its bellwether.

Of this they were conscious, and though it is not probable that they for a moment looked at the question before them with regard to this fact, it was chiefly this that prevented their seeing any alternative to the acceptance of the French. To the present day, many of the peoples of India are influenced by the same sense of their own incapacity, and it is there one of the strongest of the elements tending to the consolidation of the empire under its British rulers. As this incapacity and the belief that it is an eradicable defect of the peoples concerned has largely affected public opinion in Europe as to the present and future of the Egyptians, it will be well for us to see here to what causes it is due.

Remembering how little we can see beyond the surface of the lives, not only of our own countrymen but even of our own most intimate friends, we need not wonder that in seeking to gauge the character of a people so altogether apart from us as are the Egyptians we are apt to wander widely from the truth in our efforts to understand the ideas by which they are guided, and to be misled by giving undue weight to some feature that seems to mark them out as different from ourselves.

It is thus we find the Egyptians so commonly spoken of as "fatalists"—a term perhaps not unfairly applied as a reproach to them, but one that is too often most wrongly taken as a sufficient explanation of all their real or alleged incapacity. It is this, we are told, that has rendered them incapable of controlling their own affairs, this that has made them "the servile slaves of foreign masters." The truth is that the fatalism of the Egyptians not only plays a very small part in the framing of their characters or the guidance of their lives, but it is a fatalism of a kind not commonly understood or implied by the term. We must look elsewhere, therefore, for the explanation we need, and a slight knowledge of their history is enough to point us to the enervation caused by the system of government under which they have lived for so many centuries as at least a powerful factor in the limitation of their aptitudes.

From generation to generation deprived of all right or power of initiative, wholly without voice or influence in the affairs of the country, and habitually treated as slaves, having no other duty and owning no other privilege than that of the most perfect submission to all representing the governing power of the moment, they were of necessity entirely unaccustomed to think of or discuss any other subjects than the paltry matters of their daily lives. Yet it must not be supposed that they were debarred the liberty of speech or of comment and criticism, or that they were in any sense wholly passive victims of the tyranny from which they suffered.

Under the *beys* they from time to time "demonstrated" as loudly, if not as effectively, as our own people are wont to do. Thus, as a protest against a new impost, or, as the Tudors and Stuarts would have termed it, "Benevolence," laid upon them in the year 1794, with common consent all the business of the town was suspended, and the people went in a mass to the *cadi*, or chief justice, and the leading *ulema*, and through their intermediation obtained the revocation of the impost—for the moment, but for the moment only, for the wily *beys*, though they stormed and fumed, felt it wiser to submit and to annul the impost, but a little later substituted for it a whole series of imposts, which, being demanded at intervals and only from one or two sections of the people at a time, finally proved more profitable to the *beys* and more burthensome to the people than it would have been in its first form. It is clear, however, from this incident that the people had a fair conception of the power of united action, but the mob that marched to the *cadi's*, while it was like those of the French Revolution, leaderless, could not like those march in column, but pressed forward in a mass, a mere throng of men stirred by a common impulse.

When the Beys, to adopt a military phrase, attacked them in detail this want of leadership was fatal to their cause, and this want of leaders was due to the conditions under which the people were living, for the man who had dared to act as leader would have paid the penalty of his folly with his life, and the people would have been helpless to avenge his death. Hence anything in the nature of effective organisation or combination was impossible. Unlike their critics, the Egyptians saw then, as they do now, that without the power and opportunity of arming themselves they were, and must remain, helpless to combat the tyranny of their rulers, otherwise than by such passive means as the suspension of all trade and business.

It will be seen, then, that the condition of the Egyptians at the time of the French invasion was, in a broad way, similar to that of the Saxons under the Normans, but we need not go back to the time when Gurth bewailed the condition of his countrymen to find the masses of the English people but little better off in this respect than were the Egyptians under the Mamaluks. When in 1795 Bishop Horsley, speaking in the House of Lords, said he "did not know what the mass of the people in any country had to do with the laws but to obey them"; and the chief justice, in sentencing Muir, cried, "As for the rabble, who have nothing but personal property, what hold has the nation on them?" they might both have been speaking for the Mamaluk rulers of Egypt, and yet they spoke nothing more than the sentiment of their class.

In many other ways the condition of the English people at the close of the eighteenth century was not only not better than that of the Egyptians, but absolutely worse. In Egypt the people suffered from the *corvée*—that is to say, their liability to forced labour. In England the press-gangs dragged them from their homes for foreign service. In Egypt the people were liable to be flogged or executed on the least pretext at the whim of their rulers; in England they were subject to the same penalties by "just process of law," interpreted by such humane and benevolent persons as the two men whom I have just quoted. Let anyone who will study the records of the time with regard to the condition of the people of England, those of France, and those of Egypt, and they cannot fail to see that the advantage lay with the Egyptians.

I have elsewhere tried to show how the Egyptians looked upon the evils from which they suffered, and it must be obvious from what I have there said that this people had but little inducement to revolt. Could they have risen and annihilated the Mamaluks the only result would have been the immediate invasion of the country by a Turkish army that they could not possibly withstand and which would not fail to exact a terrible penalty from them for their temporary success.

In Egypt, then, the people had to endure much, but the ills that afflicted them were intermittent, coming upon them only now and then after longer or shorter intervals of at least comparative peace and comfort, reminding one, indeed, of the hurricanes that ravage the South Sea Islands with death and destruction, but, swiftly passing, leave the people once more to the enjoyment of the indolent, care-free life they ordinarily live.

How different had it been in France just before the Revolution! In Egypt the people always had the *ulema* to plead their cause, and if these commonly urged them to the exercise of patience and submission, they did so with a sympathy that was real. In France priest and politician alike were aloof from the people, and the evils that were crushing these were growing steadily day by day with increasing force, with no intermission, and with no possibility for a hope of better days, no possibility but one—one that found its expression in the cry of "Down with the aristocrats!"

There was no such agony of want and misery for the people of Cairo as there was for the people of Paris in those bitter days when the Revolution, unseen but with many warning mutterings, was gathering to itself the hearts of men that these might form its army of vengeance upon that "cream of civilisation" that had grown so exquisitely fine and sensitive that it had lost its natural sympathies and ceased to be conscious of its fellowship with any humanity not fitted to adorn its salons. To the Egyptian the cry of "Down with the *beys!*" would but have meant "Up with the Turks!" To the French the cry of "Down with the aristocrats!" meant "Up with myself!" and so Justice, robed in the crimson garb of Vengeance, swept over the land and, like another Frankenstein, aristocratic brutality fled from its own creation.

In England, bad as was the condition of the people, the circumstances that determined their action were very different from those that controlled the French or the Egyptians. In Egypt everything tended to discourage the people from any attempt to permanently better their condition. In France everything drove them to desperate but victorious struggle. In England the people had every incentive to action of another type. There the principle of constitutional government was recognised, and if the laws were "the most savage that ever disgraced a statute book" it was within the bounds of possibility to hope for their improvement.

The right of the people to govern themselves was not yet admitted, but their right to be heard was only denied by a class which was not beyond attack or defeat by legal means, and in the last resort rebellion was possible and by no means foredoomed to failure. The English were in the same position as the Egyptians in one respect, namely, that it was not a change in the form of government or the normal and proper condition of the people that they needed, but simply the abolition of evils that were accidental and not essential to that form or those conditions.

To the French reform had become virtually impossible. No making or mending of laws or regulations will mend the hearts of men. The *beys* of Egypt, the governing class in England, and the aristocrats in France were all heartlessly tyrannical, but the *beys* were so through capricious selfishness, the English through distorted views of justice and right, and the French through callous, persistent inhumanity. The difference in character of the tyranny under which each of the three peoples were groaning was, therefore, not less than that of their hopes for its mitigation.

The mere fact that the oppression from which he suffered was consistent with the laws of the land stirred the Englishman to hope for better things, for if he could by any means bring about a change of the laws he could not fail to benefit from it, and that such changes as he desired could be brought about he was convinced. French and Egyptians suffered not from the laws, but from the abuse of such legal authority as existed. The English, too, might, and did, hope to benefit from the mutual rivalries of the parties and classes that jointly oppressed them. The others had no such resource. And the Englishman's belief in his ability to rebel, and to rebel successfully, gave him a self-reliance and determination that everything denied to the Egyptian, and which the French could only employ in the extermination of their tyrants. Other influences were in favour of the peaceful realisation of the Englishman's hopes. He had friends in the classes above him.

There were men like Howard and Wilberforce to plead the cause of the prisoner and the slave, like Cobbett, Paine, and Wilkes to stir the people up to effort, like Burke and Pitt to preach reform, and yet more potent than all these, like Lindsey and Raikes, the founders of Sunday Schools, who, by teaching the people the value of education, laid the real foundations of the England of today, (as at time of first publication). In Egypt there were not, and could not be, such men as these. The Egyptians had, as we have seen, friends and protectors in the *ulema*, but friends whose ability to aid them was altogether out of proportion to their willingness, and whose narrow training and insufficient culture unfitted them to cope with the evils they had to face, and which many of them would have honestly laboured to amend could they but have found a way to do so.

Thus all the conditions and circumstances in the three countries tended in different directions—in one, to move the people to peaceful action; in another, to drive them to destructive wrath; and in the third, to lead them to patient submission. For the Englishman and the French, then, there were ways to progress—ways encumbered with difficulties and dangers, but with something more than a mere possibility of success to draw them onward—while the Egyptian was on all sides hemmed in by the impossible. Nor have we yet seen all the causes that have helped to determine the present character of the English and that of the Egyptians.

Then, as now, the Mahomedan peoples were taught by the *ulema*, as were, and are, the people of England by the Church Catechism, that it is their bounden duty to submit themselves to all their governors, teachers, spiritual pastors and masters, and to order themselves lowly and reverently to all their betters. But the reception accorded to this teaching by the two peoples was, and is, vastly different, and that it was and is so is mainly due to the conditions under which they are placed. The blood of the English is largely tinged with that of the restless, adventurous peoples whose early invasions of their island fill so many pages of its early history, and by descent, the influence of climate, and the whole course of their history they have become possessed of a spirit of independence, energy, and self-reliance that instinctively leads them to a broad and healthy interpretation of this doctrine.

But this spirit was altogether foreign and unknown to the Egyptian, and that it should be so was an almost inevitable result of the peculiar conditions affecting their country as contrasted with those prevailing in England. Thus in our sea-girt home, with its uncertain weather, the success of the farmer's labours was always in a great measure dependent upon his own skill and energy. Through all the changes of the seasons of the year each day brought to him its round of duties to be performed, duties exacting not only toilsome labour, but thoughtful care and wise foresight in adjusting that labour to the ever-varying conditions he had to meet. It was not so in Egypt. There the measure of the farmer's success was mainly the result of the operations of Nature, for the richness or poverty of his harvest was proportioned, not to his efforts, but to the abundance or scarcity of the inundation of the Nile.

With a bountiful flood he had little to think of but the purely routine labours of his fields; with a scanty stream no labour, no energy of his could save him from the disaster of an impoverished harvest. In England, therefore, where constant foresight, thought, and well-arranged labour were needed to win subsistence from an ungenerous soil, the farmer learned to think and act for himself, whereas in Egypt, where he was at the mercy of the Nile, he drifted on from day to day undisturbed by aught but the mere mechanically performed labour of the fields. In both countries the bent thus given to the minds of the agricultural classes with respect to their daily labour naturally affected their manner of regarding other matters.

Thus the Englishman brought to all matters that he had to deal with at least something of the care and thought he gave to his daily work, and weighed and balanced probabilities and possibilities in his political and social affairs just as he did in the choosing of a crop, while the Egyptian left almost all things to shape their own course, even as he of necessity accepted his harvest as it came. The character which the agricultural classes in the two countries thus acquired reacted upon the people generally, for it is the character of the great mass of the people that in general finally decides the character and fate of a nation.

And other causes contributed to increase the difference in the character of the two peoples. In England taxation was excessive and crushing in its effects upon all but the wealthy, but it was systematic and did not prohibit or prevent the accumulation of wealth, whereas in Egypt, while the nominal taxation was lighter it was in effect far worse, and the more so that its arbitrary assessment and irregular collection, coupled with the atrocious tyranny and cruelty by which these were accompanied, and the oft-recurring infliction of illegal taxes and impositions, effectually deprived the people of all opportunity of, or desire for, improving their position.

In England, too, labour of some kind was indispensable. Life was a constant struggle, and he who did not work was ever in imminent danger of starving. It was quite otherwise in Egypt. The grinding, hopeless poverty that not only then but still exists, though happily we may hope in an ever-lessening degree in England, was and is unknown in the East. There so few and simple are the needs of the poor that the humblest can always afford to share the little he has, and the absolute destitution, but too common in England, is there practically impossible. Moreover, the Englishman, though enjoying the benefit of a temperate climate, if he would not perish from inanition from the inclemency of its winter, was compelled to find by some means or other food of a more nourishing and stimulating quality than that which the Egyptian needed. He had also to provide himself with an amount of clothing and artificial warmth which the genial though enervating air of his native land rendered altogether unnecessary to the Egyptian. Of necessity, therefore, the Englishman's needs stirred him to an activity and energy to which the conditions of life in Egypt supplied no inducement.

Lastly, the Englishman who could acquire wealth was assured of the peaceful enjoyment of it, whereas the Egyptian knew but too well that the merest rumour of his possessing aught more than the bare necessaries of life could but subject him to tyranny and torture, until he had surrendered his last coin or seizable pennyworth of value. From this diversity in the conditions and circumstances of the two people, we can see why to the one the instruction to be content with that state of life in which he found himself was as unpalatable as to the other, it was a mere summing-up of the whole philosophy of life. However hard the condition of the Englishman's lot might be he could always look to improve it; in fact for him the one hope of happiness lay in the possibility of bettering his condition, while that of the Egyptian lay in passive submission to the chains that bound him.

That, of the two people, the Egyptian was in some respects, for the time, the happiest is at least possible. Like the Englishman, the Egyptian prizes more than all else his individual freedom: the mere liberty to come and go, to work or idle as the impulse of the moment dictates, and detests constraint and compulsion of every kind. This freedom he enjoyed with no other bar than the recurring fear of the tax-collector, the *corvée*, or the *korbag*, to which he was liable. These, however, were evils that afflicted him only at intervals, and the *corvée*, one that he always hopefully looked to escape from, while as to the *korbag*, the long strip of hippopotamus hide, which was the common instrument of punishment and extortion, ever in the hands of his oppressors, though too often used with the murderous brutality to which the negro slaves of America were then and long after subject, this would seem in general to have been to the *fellaheen* not much more terrible than was the cane of a flogging master to the boys of an English Dotheboys School of the time.

Hence his personal wants being too few and too easily supplied to give him any serious thought, the Egyptian sauntered through life on the whole contentedly enough, while the Englishman was ever ceaselessly engaged in a struggle for the bare necessaries of life; and it was as natural, therefore, for the Egyptian to accept with passive acquiescence the submission taught him by his guides, as it was inevitable that the Englishman should criticise or ignore that preached to him. Thus it was the circumstances of their lives, and not, as has so often been said, their religion, or their "fatalism," that caused the Egyptians to lack so absolutely the energy and self-reliance so dominant in the character of the Englishman, and this lack that rendered them so incapable of self-government.

That this is a correct deduction from the facts, we may see by comparing the Egyptian Moslems with the Copts, for these are of the same race, inhabit the same country, and are subject to most of the conditions of life affecting the Moslem Egyptians, and yet are essentially different from them in character and aptitude. So great and so marked is this difference that it is referred to and commented upon by everyone who has undertaken to write of Egypt and its peoples, although, apparently incapable of discovering the true origin of the contrast, those who have discussed it have either dismissed it as a problem admittedly beyond their comprehension, or have claimed that the Copt's superiority in intelligence and energy is the product of his religion. But save in matters of doctrine and dogma the religious teaching that the

Copt receives is almost exactly the same as that given to the Egyptian Moslem, with this important difference, namely, that the Copts have always considered that obedience given to a non-Christian Government is but a duty of expediency, one exacted by force and not by right, and binding upon them only so far as submission is essential to their self-preservation.

It was a matter of life and death to the Copt that he should court the forbearance and favour of his superiors. That he should do this he was bound to acquire all that he could of wealth and influence, and his relations with the rulers of the country as an indispensable servant enabled him to do this in a manner, and to an extent, wholly impossible to his Moslem countrymen.

Thus political conditions acted upon the Copt as climate and social conditions upon the Englishman, forcing him to bestir himself with energy on his own behalf, to cultivate and exercise his natural ingenuity, and trust solely in his own ability. The comparatively easygoing life of the peasant was not for him, inasmuch as he was not permitted to own land, and therefore, like the Englishman, he must either work or starve. And in doing this he had not only to compete against his fellows, but to make his way against the open hostility of the governing classes and of the people generally. Hence it is not to his religion but to the circumstances surrounding his profession of that religion that the Copt is indebted for both the good and bad characteristics by which he is distinguished, for it was these that gave him the energy, intelligence, and self-reliance he undoubtedly possesses, while at the same time they too often rendered him servile, false, bigoted, and fanatical.

It should now be clear that it is neither the "fatalism" nor the religion of the Egyptian Moslem that unfits him to govern his country. If any further evidence be wanted to justify this conclusion it is to be found in the Mamaluks and the Jews. The former, although they were Mahomedans, were by race, training, and all the circumstances of their lives, exactly opposed to the Egyptian Moslems in all their characteristics; their restless activity was strenuously employed in promoting their own interests, and in the acquisition of wealth, and in seeking these they were recklessly indifferent to the baseness of the treacheries and brutal tyranny that served their ends, and yet their religion and fatalism were the same as those of the Egyptians.

As to the Jews, these were a people suffering graver political and social disabilities than those that burthened the Copts, and wholly foreign to the Egyptian Moslem or Copt in race, habits, and aptitudes; yet under the same conditions we see them developing, not in Egypt only, but in all parts of the world, the same qualities as those of the Copts and developing them in greater or less degree, precisely as the exigencies of their surroundings control them. And as the inhabitants of towns and cities in which the struggle for existence is always keener than it is in rural districts are invariably intellectually superior to the people of those districts, so it was in Cairo, the Moslem traders and artisans, who formed the bulk of the population there, approaching the Copts in the intelligence and energy so lacking in those employed in the cultivation of the land.

I have now, I hope, shown with sufficient clearness and detail how the character and actions of the Egyptians in 1798 corresponded to the circumstances of their lives. We have been told that men should rise above their surroundings, but as I have already said, the very existence of the Egyptian depended upon his submission. The swimmer, caught in the fierce rush of a cataract, has no hope of safety but in submitting to the current and devoting all his energies to guarding himself from the rocks and eddies that are the most pressing of the dangers of his position. Such was the case with the Egyptian. To have struggled against the stream would but have been to waste his strength in futile and fatal effort, and although it was probably unconsciously that he did so, he acted in the only way to ensure the continuance of his own existence.

CHAPTER 9

The Gathering of a Storm

Cairo in 1798 as a city wherein to wander was much safer for the wanderer than was London in that year of grace. It had no Alsatia, such as Whitefriars had been in the days of Nigel, nor "Holy Land," such as the Seven Dials was down almost to our own day. It had no criminal class, and its mendicants were then as now few, and almost all strangers from elsewhere. The peaceful citizen or stranger could walk through any part of the town by day or night free from the dangers he would even today encounter if he ventured through some of the slums of the "World's Metropolis." Cairo is today unchanged from what it was in this respect save in the infamous quarter of the town devoted to the nightly carnival of vice that European civilisation demands, and, under the august protection of consuls-general and all the pomp and glory of diplomatic dignity, obtains.

Volney has drawn a sufficiently deplorable picture of the visible poverty of the Cairenes as he saw them in 1783, but it is highly probable that this glaring poverty was to a large extent of the same self-flaunting type so common in India, where certain sufficiently well-to-do classes of the people seem by their outward showing to know no mean between ostentatious prodigality and a pretence of poverty. But there was then in Cairo a class that gained its uncertain meals from still more uncertain employment, or from the hospitality or charity that in the East so seldom fails. There were, too, some waifs and wastrels, as there will always be in all great cities and towns until civilisation shall have passed its present hobbledehoy-hood.

These two classes suffered much from the total suspension of business in the town, and rendered desperate by the complete failure of all their ordinary means of livelihood, and emboldened by the absence of all authority resulting from the flight of the Mamaluks and almost all the officials and leading men of the town, broke out in lawless disorder, and, joined by many of those whom the panic-stampede had reduced to poverty, began pillaging the deserted houses and mansions of all that was left in them.

Bonaparte being informed of this, at once sent parties of soldiers into the town with the double object of suppressing outrage and robbery and of seizing everything of value that the Mamaluks and other fugitives had been forced by the haste of their departure to leave behind them. Proclamation was also made that whatever had been taken by any person from any of the deserted houses should at once be surrendered to the French, and, as a warning to those who might be inclined to disobey this command, several men who were caught either in the act of stealing or in the possession of stolen property were summarily executed. Not content with these measures for the recovery and protection of what he no doubt regarded as his lawful booty, Bonaparte is said to have countenanced, if he did not actually order, the infliction of torture with a view to forcing the disclosure of hidden wealth.

The prompt and energetic steps taken by the French quickly restored order in the town, and this having been done Bonaparte began to take in hand the work of introducing civilisation as it was then understood in France. Like the common type of "Reformer" and "Philanthropist," in doing this he effectually barred the way to the success of his efforts by coupling his professions of friendship for the people with conditions. It was a case of "Be my brother, or I will slay you." He was going to render the people for ever happy and content beyond their dreams, but they, on their part, must yield the most implicit obedience to all that seemed necessary or advisable to him. They were to have cake and apples like the good children in the nursery tale, but, like them, they must all sit in a row and behave nicely—in the French fashion, which at least was appropriate, since the cakes and apples they were promised were all of the latest fashion from Paris itself.

It is rather a pitiable picture that the "Little Corporal" makes, thus playing the part of a glorified Bumble with "Civilisation" and other fallacious figments for his "parochial" board, and the porridge bowl of "the house" filled with "Liberty, Equality, and Fraternity," to be doled out in duly measured spoonfuls to the hungry and needy. Poor Cairenes! like the hungry Oliver they were to take what they got and be thankful, and not mutinously set up a standard of their own. They were not only to be fed but feasted. They were to remain good Mahomedans, be free in all respects, and be most happy and prosperous but—they must wear the cockade, and shout "*Vive la République*" in such French or Arabic as they could. So, as a foretaste of the banquet to which they were invited, fair words and fine promises were lavishly scattered among them, but not without a liberal seasoning of orders, warnings, and threats. For a short time all went well, but it was not very long before the people began to think that the seasoning was somewhat out of proportion to the rest of the dish.

In the time of the *beys*, which within a week seemed to the Cairenes to have grown old and distant, the streets of the town had been swept and watered by day and lit by night, but, like everything else good and useful in those days, these things had been done in a manner that left much to be desired. As the town settled slowly back to its old round of life, if left to themselves the people would, undoubtedly, have renewed these and others of their ancient customs; but these were matters in which French propriety could brook no delay, and orders were therefore issued that sweeping, watering, and lighting should at once be brought into play.

To this no objection would have been taken had the order stopped there; unfortunately it is a virtuous vice of the French to love precision—a quality which the Egyptian appreciates only when applied to the attainment of grammatical purity in the use of the Arabic language, but which, being otherwise repugnant to his spirit, is not to be found in his native dialect or everyday speech or thought, and still less in more important matters. Hence when the French, in obedience to their natural impulse, fixed times and methods and degrees for the sweepings and waterings and lightings they demanded from the people, and enforced the orders by the proclamation of pains and penalties to be inflicted upon defaulters, and, moreover, did all this without consulting anyone as to the native customs and recognised conventions applicable to such matters, there was much grumbling.

Thus the lighting of the streets by night was ordered on a scale that made it a real grievance, for each and every house was commanded to hang out upon its outer wall not a banner but a lamp—a prodigality of illumination that the Cairene looked upon as utterly unprofitable. Very primitive were the lamps available in those days. In London itself ladies returning in their chairs at night from balls and routs, and not improbably bemoaning the damage done to their attire by drippings from the spluttering candles of the ballroom they had left, were lighted on their way by linkmen carrying torches.

And since even the Beau Brummels of those days had to put up with such primitive forerunners of the incandescent lights that today seem to us as indispensable for comfort, it is not surprising that the honest citizen of Cairo, when delayed from home until after dark, was content to be accompanied by a servant carrying a small, rudely made lamp set in a lantern of paper—a custom that survives to the present day in the *harahs*, or back streets of the native town, though now the lamps used are lit by Russian oil and sheltered from the wind in lanterns of Austrian glass. But when every reputable man who went through the town at night had his lantern-bearer with him there was not much need for the lighting of the streets in a more general way, and so the Cairenes had been satisfied to consider a street well lighted if it had a lamp hung out here and there at longer or shorter intervals to serve rather as a beacon than as a light.

A lamp to every house was to them, therefore, an absurd extravagance, and when householders were further made responsible, under penalty of a fine, not only for the placing and lighting of the lamps, but also for seeing that they were kept alight throughout the night, this, to the French idea, most judicious measure became to the Cairenes a very real grievance and one that worried and annoyed all classes.

To provide for the administration of the affairs of the town generally, and to act as an intermediary between the French and the people, a *dewan* was constituted similar to that which had already been established at Alexandria. This consisted of ten Sheikhs, who appear to have been chosen principally as being those most openly opposed to the Mamaluks. But on the urgent representations of the leading men, that the Turks or Mamaluks were the only men in the country accustomed to, or capable of, exercising efficient authority, Bonaparte very unwillingly appointed three or four Mamaluk officials who had remained in the town to different posts; and several Frenchmen were added, nominally to co-operate with, but in reality to control, the native members of the *dewan*.

Notwithstanding the assurances thus given to the people, that it was the intention of the French to carry on the government with all respect to their religion and customs, the merchants and dealers showed some reluctance to reopening their shops and stores. When, however, the troops mixing freely with the people, as we have seen, and abstaining from the violence and injustice that it had always been the experience of the townsmen to receive at the hands of the followers of the *beys*, confidence was restored, not only was the former trade of the town resumed, but shops, especially intended for the benefit and service of the French, were started.

Meanwhile, the expedition having been accompanied by a body of scientific experts, who had been instructed to prepare the most detailed and elaborate accounts of everything that could throw light upon the state of the country and its people, and the capacity of each for development, these men were set to work, each with a definite task to fulfil. Furnished with quarters in the deserted mansions of the fugitive *beys*, they at once commenced the labours which were to give to the world the vast, though unhappily incomplete, description of Egypt, which is unquestionably the most marvellous work of the kind ever undertaken. Of these men it may be said that they represented all that is best and noblest in the French nation and the higher aspirations of the revolution.

But however eager Bonaparte was to restore order in Cairo and to promote the scientific, commercial, and colonising objects of the expedition, his strongest desires and ambitions lay in another direction, and he began therefore to prepare for further action. That he might do this with the greater ease he resolved upon two steps, which tended not a little to diminish the contentment of the people with his rule. The first of these was a demand for money presented to the *dewan*, which was instructed to collect the stipulated amount from the whole community, Christian and Jewish as well as Moslem. To this, though not without demur, the Dewan consented; but the announcement of the impost that was to be raised was to the people the betrayal of the cloven hoof, and although it was a measure they had been fearing, and which, had it been imposed upon them immediately after the arrival of the French in the city, would have been accepted as a natural exercise of the prerogative of a conqueror, was now looked upon as a breach of faith, and as such completely destroyed confidence in the fair words and promises of the French.

The discontent and uneasiness thus occasioned gave birth to open and evident dismay and agitation when the second measure taken by Bonaparte was announced. From its first building, the town had been divided into *harahs* or quarters—districts separated from each other by the run of the streets, and by walls and gates. These gates it was the custom to close soon after sunset, and thereafter no one was allowed to pass from one quarter to another without the permission of the watchmen charged with the care of the gates. In thus dividing the town its founders had two main objects in view—one, by the separation of the inhabitants into a number of clearly defined groups, to be able to fix responsibility for crime on a particular group; and the other that, in the event of a mutiny or rebellion, the closing of the gates might serve to isolate the various groups from each other, and thus facilitate the work of the government in dealing with them. Bonaparte, however, far from thinking the existence of the *harahs* as contributing to the maintenance of order, regarded them as affording dangerous shelter to malcontents, and resolved to abolish them.

Parties of soldiers were therefore set to work to remove the gates. As soon as the people became aware of this the most alarming rumours were circulated, such as that this was being done to enable the French to carry out a wholesale massacre of the people, either by night or when they should be assembled in the mosques for the special prayers of the Friday noon, which at that time it was the pride, as well as it still is the duty, of all Moslems to attend. So great was the alarm of the people at this idea that the newly opened shops were closed once more, and business, which had been growing as brisk as it was profitable, was again suspended; but nothing occurring to justify their fears, the alarm passed, and the bazaars, that for the moment had been more or less deserted, again began to fill with life and animation.

As was but natural, the arrival of the French had from the first been hailed with delight by the Christian population. Under the Mamaluks these, whether native or foreign, had suffered from many disabilities, and, though rarely openly molested by the Moslems, were at all times subject to the insults and rudenesses of the lower classes. Now, under the protection of the French, they threw off the restraints to which they had so long submitted, and excited the anger of the Moslems by appearing in public in the silk and gold-embroidered costumes that had been forbidden to them under the Mamaluks. *Cafés*, restaurants, and wine-shops were opened by the Greeks and others, and wine was sold and drunk in public, to the great indignation of the *ulema* and all the better class of the Moslems.

These and other things, of little moment in themselves, became important factors in modifying the feelings of the people towards the French, by marking the change in the relative standing of the followers of the two religions, and by largely discounting the professions of friendship for the Moslem faith with which Bonaparte endeavoured to conciliate the goodwill of the Mahomedans.

Many other causes helped to keep the people from settling down quietly under the French. Among these was the constant searching of houses for arms or valuables belonging to the Mamaluks, and the arrest and imprisonment of those suspected or accused of concealing wealth or property of any kind on their behalf. One of those who suffered directly in this way was the wife of Radwan Kachef who had fled with Ibrahim Bey. This lady had paid a sum of one thousand three hundred dollars to the French as reconciliation money, in consideration of which she had been granted the right to remain in Cairo under French protection.

A few days afterwards, a report having reached Bonaparte that her husband had left a quantity of arms and money in her care, a search was made, and some clothing, arms, and other things being found, all the women in the house were arrested and a fine of four thousand dollars imposed upon the lady as the condition of their release. Had the French been content to seize the arms no objection would have been taken to their action, but the fine was, in the eyes of all the people, a breach of faith.

If thus rigorous with the Mahomedan population, Bonaparte made it plain that he had no intention of unduly favouring the Christians. On the 2nd of August Nelson, having returned to Alexandria, had, in the famous battle of the Nile, destroyed the French fleet, and the army in Egypt was thus cut off from all communication with Europe and left entirely dependent upon itself. News of this event having been brought to Cairo, the Moslems were as elated as the French and Christians were depressed. Bonaparte at once instituted a search for the persons who had first made the ill news known, and these proving to be two Syrian Christians and a Moslem, all three were condemned to have their tongues cut out or pay a heavy fine.

This was in every way a foolish measure. It had the effect of checking the open discussion of reports unfavourable to the French, who, by adopting this ostrich-like policy, deprived themselves of the only method they had of gauging the tendency of public opinion, and, while they could not thus prevent the dissemination of news or rumours, gave the people a fresh and reasonable grievance, for under even the most tyrannical of the rulers they had previously known they had been allowed a liberty of speech that it was clear was now to be denied them, and the distrust of the fair words that Bonaparte was so lavish in offering them was still further increased.

Nor did the punishment of the Christians impress the Mahomedans with any sense of the impartiality that Bonaparte intended it to convey, for it was regarded as nothing more than the wreaking of his anger, at the bad news received, upon those who, Christian or not, were, according to popular opinion, guiltless of any real offence. It was thus an act such as they were accustomed to expect from the Mamaluks, and, in the eyes of the Cairenes, placed the boasted justice and humanity of the French on the same level as those of the *beys*.

As time went on almost every day brought some fresh incident to swell the stream of ill-feeling towards the French that Bonaparte, in his self-sufficient direction of affairs, was creating. Had he but acted with some little consideration for the wishes of the people, and consulted their prejudices, it is certain that the storm that was now rapidly approaching would never have arisen. But Bonaparte was never able to get beyond the nursery policy of cake or cane. There was no worse policy open to him. Neither with cake nor with cane was it possible to persuade or drive the Cairenes to adopt his views. By a ceaseless play of petty tyranny he was able to force from them an unwilling compliance with his demands, but every little victory thus gained served to widen the gulf between the two peoples, and thus to defeat that which any man of real ability would have seen was the aim that of all others it was the interest of the French to pursue—the conciliation of the Egyptians.

While thus blundering along, baffling his own desires, Bonaparte, always believing in his own tact and good judgment, decided to give his patronage to the annual ceremony of the Cutting of the *khalig*, or canal, that from the time of the Pharaohs has been held in Cairo in celebration of the flooding of the Nile. In the old heathen days this had been essentially a festival of thanksgiving to the gods, but as the greatest and most popular feast of the year it had survived the conversion of the people to Christianity and Islam and was kept as a day of merry-making upon which the people gave unrestricted play to their tireless love of gaiety. But the Moslems were in no mood to join in revelry when Bonaparte summoned them to do so, and though the French have recorded the occasion as one of unbounded success the fact is that it was far otherwise.

It was the same with the celebration of the *molid*, or birthday of the Prophet, that occurred soon after. This being in its first inception a religious feast, had, like the wakes and feasts of the saints of Christendom, long been accompanied by revelries and rejoicings of a most unsaintly character, and was, to the Moslem population of Cairo, the great event of the year, the pious celebrating it with prayer and praise and the *zikrs*—that would seem to be an Islamic adaptation of the

94

ancient worship of the Israelites when they sang songs unto the Lord with timbrels and harps—while others less piously inclined spent the night in carousings and sports. But whether pious or otherwise the Moslems of Cairo had no desire to hold the feast of their Prophet under the auspices of the Christian invader, and the anniversary would have been allowed to pass unnoticed but that the Sheikh Sadat, the recognised head of the family of the descendants of the Prophet living in Egypt, fearing that Bonaparte would take the refusal to hold it in bad part, gave the order for its celebration, and invited the general and his staff to be present.

So, wholly blind to the storm that was gathering, and flattering himself that what he deemed a wise combination of firmness and conciliation was gradually building up a strong tower of French influence in the country, Bonaparte went on from day to day holding out his cakes and cane temptingly or threateningly, much as a silly old woman dangles a gaudy trinket or calls for the bogie-man to coax or terrify a restless child. For the cakes the Egyptians had no appetite whatever, and for the cane, since they could see no way to escape from its unwelcome favours, they were content to pray for an early deliverance from the French and all their abominations.

Some days after the celebration of the *molid*, Bonaparte, having invited the leading *sheikhs* to visit him, prepared for them what he probably thought would prove an agreeable surprise. Receiving his guests with the affability he generally displayed, he retired to an adjoining room, and presently returned with a number of tricolour sashes and cockades. With a smile that was meant to be winning and gracious, he put one of these across the shoulder of the Sheikh el Sharkawi, the President of the *dewan*. Flushing red with fury, the *sheikh* flung the sash upon the ground. With hurried but soothing words the interpreter sought to explain that the sash was intended as a mark of honour—that it was one of those worn by the general himself—and added that by wearing it the *sheikh* would gain increased respect from the army.

"Yes," replied the *sheikhs*, "but we should be dishonoured in the eyes of God and of our co-religionists!" Here was a sudden flood of mutiny indeed! The tricolour, emblem of all that was honourable, sacred, flung to the ground as though it were an unclean and unholy thing, not to mention the rough discourtesy to the general. What wonder if Bonaparte, as the histories tell us, was "furious" or "enraged"? Was it not exasperating to be taught in this rude manner that the everyday politeness and conciliating manner of these wretched Egyptian *sheikhs* really had limits, and that there was a point beyond which they would not go? And the humiliation of having offered a favour only to have it rejected with scorn, and that by men whose very lives depended upon his forbearance!

Poor Bonaparte! How many things there were in heaven and earth that were not dreamt of in his philosophy! And poor Sharkawi! Quick as was the ready-witted interpreter to interpose his well-meant explanation, I am well convinced that he was not quick enough to forestall the *sheikh's* audible or inaudible cry for forgiveness for such hasty and unseemly anger. But, audible or inaudible, his cry was not to the general, but to the God to whom, as the Moslem believes, anger and hasty speech are abominations. The general, being restrained by no such considerations, and having, we may admit, much more reason to be enraged than the *sheikh*, broke forth in an angry denunciation of the worthy President of the *dewan* as one entirely unfitted for the high and honourable post he held, and had his wrath increased rather than soothed by the polite endeavours of the *sheikhs* to pacify him, while at the same time begging him not to press the sashes upon them.

At length he yielded so far as to withdraw the sashes, but continued to demand the wearing of the cockade, believing, no doubt, like young Easy's nurse, that this, being such a little one, would be a more pardonable offence against outraged propriety. But the *sheikhs* were as little willing to wear the cockade as they were to put on the sash, reasonably arguing that it was not the size of the emblem but its meaning and purport that was objectionable. Finally, when the question had been discussed with much good sense and much folly on both sides, it was agreed that the *sheikhs* should have some days' grace wherein to consider and decide the issue.

On the same day proclamation was made throughout the town to the effect that all the people were to put on the cockade and wear it as a sign of submission and amity. A few only consented, but the opposition of the majority was so strong that later in the day the order was withdrawn, with the condition that all who should have any business with the French, or visited their houses or quarters, should don the despised decoration for the occasion. Here, then, the incident ended, but we must not wholly dismiss it without noticing that Gabarty and others of the *sheikhs*, although they were not willing to wear the French colours, were quite clear in their opinion that doing so was no offence to Moslem law or sentiment. It was simply a silly fad of the French, without any real meaning or sense. Whence it is obvious that what is spoken of as progressive or enlightened thought in Islam has not altogether resulted from the influence of European or Christian civilisation, but is the natural product of the freedom of thought inherent in the teaching of the religion.

Learning nothing from the experience that would have taught an abler man the weakness and strength of his position, Bonaparte was thus gradually, though wholly unwittingly, driving the people to rebellion. Misreading the passive acceptance or mild protests with which his rapidly succeeding mandates were received, he kept on, from day to day, more hopelessly and more completely widening the gulf already yawning between the two peoples, and while daily outraging the Egyptians' conception of liberty and happiness, never ceased to talk of the benefits he was conferring upon them, or to wonder at their failure to appreciate all the charm and beauty of the changes he was so anxious to promote.

Under the Mamaluks the people had had but three grievances to complain of, and one of these, the destruction of commerce and trade, they only partly, if at all, attributed to the fault of their rulers. The other two were the excessive taxation to which they were subjected, and the acts of more or less wanton cruelty and oppression that classes as well as individuals were liable to. Apart from these things, their lives were as free as they could desire. They worked or idled, came and went, and, in short, did all things as they listed under no greater restraint than that of the lenient opinion of their fellows, which even when most censorious, was still prone to the Moslem virtue of forgiveness. Little by little Bonaparte went on encroaching upon these liberties the people had always possessed and prized. Births, marriages, and deaths had to be recorded, and fees had to be paid to the recording officers.

Those entering the town had to give an account of themselves, whence they came and why. Those who received visitors or strangers in their houses were responsible for them. Those who wished to travel or leave the town had to provide themselves with passports. These and a host of other regulations that, to the French, seemed but natural and proper parts of the organisation of a State, were to the Egyptians intolerable outrages upon their personal liberty, and that nothing should be wanting to make these reforms unpopular, each was fitted with a fee of some sort, to be paid upon demand, with dire pains and penalties for all omissions or defaults of any kind.

It is difficult for the ordinary Englishman or European to form any intelligent or just conception of the feelings of irritation to which these measures gave rise, but those who have travelled in Russia and have there experienced something of the wrath its passport regulations can arouse in the breast of a freeborn Briton, may perhaps be able to imagine how the imposition of such restrictions by a foreign conqueror in his own house would affect him. If he can do this the reader can form some slight idea of the feelings with which the Egyptians regarded the "reforms" they were forced to accept and asked to admire and applaud. But it was not their personal grievances that rankled most deeply in the hearts of the people, or most surely crushed all possibility of sympathy or friendship between them and their new rulers.

Among the incidents that most strongly affected the people was the execution of Sayed Mahomed Kerim, the man whom, as we have seen, Bonaparte had left as Governor at Alexandria. Accused by the French of corresponding with the Mamaluks, he was sent up to Cairo for such trial as he was to have, and was promptly sentenced to pay a heavy fine or, in default, to suffer death. That he was guilty of the offence appears certain, and according to all known laws of war, he was therefore guilty of a breach of parole and liable to death. But the offence that Sayed Kerim had committed was, in fact, nothing more than a technical one, since it consisted in his having offered to admit the Mamaluks to Alexandria while these, so far from being in a position to occupy that town, had abandoned all attempts to face the French.

Bonaparte and his army were no doubt present in Egypt as conquerors, but the foe had not only been beaten but cowed, the people of the country had made the fullest submission, and it was an abuse of terms to pretend that there was the slightest pretext to justify the application of the laws of war. The option of a fine granted to Sayed Kerim shows indeed that Bonaparte recognised this fact, and at the same time proves his utter incapacity to gauge the sentiments of the people or realise their estimate of his actions. Moreover, according to the popular view, Sayed Kerim was guilty of no offence whatever, for his promise of fealty to the French was not made voluntarily, and therefore was not binding.

Some looked upon his sentence as a proof that the French were afraid of the return of the Mamaluks, others held that the charge had been brought simply to provide the French with an excuse for the seizure of the Sayed's property. All their sympathies were therefore with

1. This chapter is composed of unfinished notes from Mrs. Gamewell's pen.

the prisoner, and they were enhanced a thousandfold by the fact that he was a descendant of the Prophet. But Bonaparte, for all his fulsome speeches to the people, cared nothing for their wishes or desires, and it was in vain that the *ulema* and all who could obtain a hearing pleaded for at least a mitigation of the sentence. Bonaparte would hear no reason. The full fine must be paid at once or the prisoner must die.

But the Sayed was defiant. "Of what use," said he, "is it that I should pay the fine? If it is my destiny to die I must die, and no fine can save me, and if it is not my destiny to die, who can slay me?" So he died as one expects such a man to die, openly defying his foes, and Bonaparte had his head carried through the town, with written and verbal proclamation that such was the fate that awaited all who conspired against the French, little recking that the lesson he intended this gruesome performance to be was taken by the people in a very different manner to that which he desired, and so far from being a lesson of submission and obedience, was one of hatred and vengeance.

From the European point of view it is, of course, impossible to censure Bonaparte for his treatment of Sayed Kerim. In matters of this kind European civilisation was in those days very little better than the East. It is true that in England traitors' heads no longer provided the public with an interesting spectacle on Tower Hill, but "My Lord Tom Noddy," and the smart set of that day, highly appreciated the entertainment afforded by the hanging of miserable prisoners sentenced to death for petty thefts, or even for attempting to steal, and the bones of highwaymen still hung in chains on the heaths around London, startling unwary nightfarers with their unwelcome rattle.

So Bonaparte went blundering on. Failing entirely to grasp the position, and fancying that he was laying the foundations of that great Eastern Empire of which he dreamed, he was blindly ignorant of and indifferent to the one and only means whereby he could succeed, for if it had been possible for him to realise his dream it could only have been by gaining the adhesion of the Egyptians as his first step. That he could have done this I do not believe, but it was absolutely the only possible road to success open to him, and it was the one that in the futile folly of his overweening confidence in himself and his methods he would not or could not adopt. He might have gone far on the road. Had he left the people at rest, had he respected in fact and deed as in words he professed to do, their prejudices and desires, had he gained as he might have gained the passive if not active support of the *ulema*— had he done these things, nothing but a greatly superior force could have dislodged him from Egypt.

But these were the very things that he did not do. As we have seen, instead of giving the people the rest from tyranny and vexations for which they longed, he harassed them infinitely more than the worst of all the rulers that had preceded him. So with the *ulema*, instead of seeking their friendship in the only way in which it was to be obtained, he mocked them with idle pretences of respect that were never justified by deeds, and, while loudly declaring his respect for Islam and its teaching, ignored both in the most offensive way, and thus not only offended the people, but completely barred himself from the support of the *ulema*. So keeping his way with dogged will and unbroken faith in his own ability, he was blindly though surely swelling the tide of discontent fast rising around him, and soon to burst forth in stormy wrath.

CHAPTER 10

The Bursting of the Storm

Looking back now we can see that as the month of September drew to a close the gathering of clouds betokening the growing storm was becoming more and more evident. But the French were altogether unconscious of anything being wrong. That the Egyptians were woefully wanting in gratitude, and most strangely incapable of appreciating the benefits that were being showered upon them—this they saw plain enough. Nor were they blind to the fact that flaunt the tricolour as bravely as they would, the liberty, equality, and fraternity it symbolised were flouted by this people, whose whole history was a record of slavery and degradation. But they did not see that they themselves were hated and detested, that the cordiality with which for a time the people had fraternised with the soldiers had been but a passing reaction, and that, sincere as it was for the moment, it could not continue.

The French in Cairo were then, as Europeans in the East almost always are, quite content to see the surface of the life around them. Of its hidden depths they knew nothing, and therefore judged the strangers amidst whom they were wholly by their own standards. It is but little better today, (as at time of first publication). In Egypt, as in India, everything "native" is despised, not because it is native, nor yet that it is bad, but because it is not such as the critical European has been accustomed to, and is therefore not "good form." To stop and ask whether the native may not have good sense, and be acting with good reason in doing as he does, never occurs to the self-satisfied European. So, having the power to do so, we thrust our misbegotten "reforms" upon the people, scorn these for not appreciating our absurdities, and despise them for not applauding our follies.

We talk of the Egyptian as backward, bigoted, and prejudiced. A falser charge could not be brought against any people. From highest to lowest, among the most "fanatical" as among the most lax and liberal, the Egyptian takes and adopts as his own whatever he finds good in the ways of other peoples. Nowhere is there a people of greater adaptability, nowhere a people more ready or more willing to accept innovations. Nor is there in all the East a people who has the same, or anything like the same, silly self-sufficiency as the typical Englishman in the East. Other Europeans are bad enough in this respect, but none fall near so low in the scale of common sense as does the Englishman.

But if the Egyptian is willing to accept innovations he is stubbornly insistent upon accepting them in his own manner. He is not willing to have them forced upon him, nor to accept those that clash with his cherished prejudices, nor those that do not commend themselves to him as beneficial, and he demands, further, that whatever change he is asked to adopt is made smoothly and without any abrupt or violent alteration of old-established custom or habit. All these conditions were violated day after day by the French. The reforms they introduced were opposed to all the traditions of the country. They disturbed the habits of the people, interrupted the current of their old-time routine, offended their prejudices, and were forced upon them suddenly and as peremptory mandates demanding immediate and unquestioning obedience. Had they been allowed to criticise and discuss each new proposal they might, being as fond as old Mr. Easy himself of arguing the question, have been won by patience and tact to accept most of them.

So as time went on, and the people had abundant scope for comparisons between French promises and French performances, they were not without reason in accusing them of the faithlessness that the Turks have stamped as their characteristic in the rhyming phrase, "*Fransiz imansiz.*" Still, though daily finding fresh cause of grievance against the French, the people were outwardly submissive, and it did not occur to the French that their pacific attitude could be otherwise than willing. So far, indeed, they were right—it was willing, but the cause of its being so was very different to that which the French assumed it to be, for it is clear that these believed that this willingness was due partly to the people's acceptance of their professions of friendship and partly to their inability to resist. But the submissiveness of the Egyptians had a very different origin.

They knew that news of the arrival of the French had been despatched to Constantinople from Cairo almost as soon as it had been received there, and they were certain that the events that followed, the defeat of the Mamaluks and the seizure of Cairo by the French, had also been communicated to the *sultan*, and they were therefore looking forward from day to day to the coming of a Turkish army, and never for a moment fancied that the French occupation would or could be other than a temporary one. These things were discussed freely and fully enough in the houses of the people, but the French, as we have seen, had deliberately closed the only door by which a knowledge of the real sentiments and feelings of the people could reach them. To speak of a French disaster or defeat was a punishable treason, and so the Cairenes, doing violence to their natural inclinations, held their tongues in public, only to talk the more and the more bitterly in their homes. Nor did the Egyptians look upon the Mamaluks as having been finally and decisively beaten.

French troops had now been in pursuit of the fugitive *beys* for some months, and though the French were careful to publish everything that could be made to redound to the glory and credit of their arms, they had not yet been able to record any success worthy of note or which was not discounted by the facts reaching the people from other sources. Nor had the severity with which Bonaparte had punished those who were convicted of circulating the news of the destruction of the French fleet failed to impress the Cairenes with the great importance they attached to that event, or to increase their hopes of the early and utter destruction of the French army. To the Egyptians, therefore, the ultimate disappearance of the French was only a question of time, and situated as they were it is not surprising that they bore the miseries the occupation was inflicting upon them with the outward semblance of content that so misled the French.

Towards the middle of September a Turkish eunuch arrived from Constantinople, and the people, believing that he was the bearer of letters from the *sultan*, flocked in thousands after him as he passed through the streets. Bonaparte happened just then to be in the town, whither he had gone to pay a visit to one of the leading Sheikhs, and returning came in sight of the crowd following the new arrival. Instantly loud cries broke forth, maledictions on the French, mingled with shouts of "Victory to the *Sultan*" and to Islam. Wholly unable to comprehend the meaning of the demonstration, since it was the habit of the people to receive him in silence, he asked what it meant, and was told that the people were acclaiming his presence. "It was," says Gabarty, "a critical moment, and one that might have had grave consequence." One can but wonder that the incident passed as harmlessly as it did, for it is certain that in the temper the people were in it needed but a word to have stirred them to action. Fortunately for Bonaparte the dangerous moment passed, and he was left to return home with no suspicion of how narrowly he had escaped an ignoble ending of his career.

A few days later the French held high festival in honour of the anniversary of the Republic. A great space in the Esbekieh was chosen as the site of the rejoicings, and this was encircled with Venetian poles swathed in the colours so dear to French sentiment, and linked together with festooned flowers. A triumphal arch decorated with frescoes celebrating the defeat of the Mamaluks, was erected in the centre, and on all sides French and Turkish flags were displayed in profusion. The Cap of Liberty and the Turkish Crescent, the "Rights of Man" and the *Koran*, the glory of the Prophet and that of the French Republic, were inextricably mixed up in the decorations as emblems of the hopes of the French, but were in truth more aptly typical of the absolute irreconcilability of the two peoples assembled in their presence.

In the evening there was a grand banquet, to which all the principal *sheiks* and other leaders of the people were invited, and at which speeches of great length, but light and witty, full of the spirit that the French seem always to have at command, were made, and the night was brought to a close with a display of fireworks, after which the French went home to sigh for the early coming of the day on which they could return to their beloved France, and the Egyptians to pray for the coming of that same day, but for very different reasons and with very different hopes.

Needless to say that the *fête* was made an opportunity for the renewal of all the fine promises and a gorgeous repainting of all the brilliant prospects that Bonaparte was never weary of holding out to the Egyptians; but the *fête* over, he pursued his policy of reform more vigorously and more recklessly than ever. A new scheme for the registration of property was introduced, taxes were imposed upon the inheritance of property, on creditors' claims, on hirings and lettings, and a host of other things. All the citizens living in the citadel were turned out, speaking of politics was forbidden, arrests, confiscations, and executions went on from day to day, the cemeteries within the city walls were closed, and the disinfecting of the houses and clothing of the dead was ordered. These, and a host of other innovations, each in its way reasonable enough, and, according to modern European ideas, most commendable, came upon the Egyptians as ruthless invasions of their personal liberty, and were viewed by them as tyrannical expedients for robbing them.

And with these measures for the social organisation of the town Bonaparte was pressing forward others for its defence, for in spite of his suppression of speech among the people he was becoming aware of the fact that they were looking for the coming of a foe to dispute possession of the country with him, and an infinitely more deadly foe than Turk or Mamaluk was already within the walls of the city, and was not to be combated or ousted by any means that he could command; a foe that mocked the might of generals and armies, and in the stillness of a night might decimate the French troops; a foe whose very name—the plague—blanched the faces and hearts of every European who heard it.

So, that the army as a whole, or whatever fraction of it the plague might spare, should be in a condition to defend itself from the assaults of Turk or Mamaluk, the French put feverish haste in the building of defences, and houses, mansions, tombs, and mosques were pulled down to make room for and supply materials for forts and other works. Meanwhile the *dewan* had not answered Bonaparte's expectations, and as the almost necessary result it was neglected. It met from time to time, to disperse again without having had any affairs presented for its consideration, and the people drawing their own conclusions from all that was going on, adding this to other matters, with a steadily rising tide of anger in their hearts, drew more and more apart from the French, and these apparently began to have some suspicion that all was not going on so well as they could wish.

October came, and a new *dewan* was formed with delegates from Alexandria and other towns as members. Then a new law of succession was proposed, as though the French were determined to leave nothing undone that would serve to prove how utterly blind they were in the folly with which they were pushing the people to desperation. The law of succession that then, as now, prevailed in Egypt, as in all Moslem lands and amongst all Moslem peoples, is based upon the express injunctions of the *Koran*, and being therefore, as all Moslems believe, conformable to the direct command of God Himself, the mere suggestion to modify or alter it in any way whatever is an unpardonable offence.

Yet that the madness with which the French were acting should be still more emphatically proved, not only was the proposed new law of succession absolutely and utterly rejected by the Moslems, but also by the Christians and Jews, who declared that sooner than have it they would prefer the Moslem law. Once more, then, Bonaparte had to suffer the humiliation of withdrawing a hasty and ill-conceived measure. The people would no more have his law of succession than his cockades. But still hopelessly incapable of comprehending the real nature of the task he was so fatuitously pursuing, he only consented to abandon this scheme to introduce another not less detestable to the whole population. This was a proposal for a house-tax, and it was to the Cairenes the spark that set aflame the fiercely smouldering fires a hundred others had kindled.

So far the people had contented themselves with verbal protests, and even these had been so infrequent and so moderate in tone that the French may almost be excused for misreading the submissive, all-bearing attitude with which the great majority of their innovations were accepted, and for believing that the people were incapable of any more effective resistance. They were now to learn by evidence that could not be gainsaid that it was no cowardly fear that had dictated their passiveness. It was not the first time that the Cairenes were to give a proof that they could act in their own defence when they chose to do so, but it was the first since the arrival of the French, and it served to show that, like that of a finely tempered spring when released from restraint, the pliancy of their temper but rendered its reaction sharper and stronger. A fiery, quarrelsome people would have broken out against the French a dozen times while yet the Egyptian was silently submitting to his wrongs, but their outbreaks would not have had the weight or force of that which was now to interrupt and change the whole relations of the vanquished and the vanquishers.

According to custom, the newly proposed house-tax was made known to the people by printed copies of the decree concerning it being posted all over the town. On the whole it was a moderate and most inoffensive measure, and one that trespassed less on the prejudices of the Cairenes than did many of those that had preceded it. The private houses and dwellings of the town were to be grouped in three classes according to their value. The first and highest class was to pay eight, the second six, the third three dollars a year. Dwellings let at less than a dollar a month were to be exempt. Shops, public baths, *cafés*, and other buildings for the accommodation of the public were rated at from thirty to forty dollars. Many of the people accepted this fresh burthen without any special comment, looking upon it as but one straw more of the heavy load being laid upon them; but others grumbled, less at the tax itself than at the principle involved in its application. Some of the *sheikhs* lending their support to this latter party, it quickly developed itself, and the angry malcontents, without any very definite plan or accepted leader, began to arm themselves with the weapons that, in spite of all the efforts of the French to disarm the population, they had kept hidden away in their houses and elsewhere.

It was a Sunday morning, but as neither the French nor the Cairenes at that time paid any respect to the day, the city wore its everyday aspect, until the discontented began to gather, and with loud cries of "Victory for Islam!" set out for the house of the *cadi*. Alarmed at the approach of the turbulent mob, and having no clear knowledge of its aims, the *cadi* hastened to have his doors closed and refused admission to the rioters. Enraged at the reception given them by the man who of all others they regarded as their natural and proper leader, the people, without a moment's hesitation, attacked the house, shattering its windows with stones picked up from the street.

In this attack upon the *cadi's* house we have a clear measure of the wrath that was stirring the people, for the *cadi*, the chief of the *ulema*, chief justice of the country, and the local supreme orthodox authority of the Moslem faith and law, sent from Constantinople as the representative and exponent of the spiritual authority vested in the *sultan* as the *caliph* of Islam, was and is to the Egyptian almost as a cardinal is to the followers of "that most fascinating of all superstitions," as Macaulay styled the Catholic Church. As the hustling, shouting horde of rioters approached the *cadi's* house the whole fate of the day was placed in his hands, for, as he must have known, they were approaching him that he might become their leader and mouthpiece, it being thus that they had been accustomed to make their protests against the tyrannies and exactions of the *beys*.

A most ingenious and effective diplomatic wile, for the people thus presented themselves to the *beys* under the sheltering patronage of the *cadi*, whose definite decision the hardiest of the *beys* would not dare to openly dispute, while the *cadi* himself could plead that he was acting under compulsion and yet give the claims of the people such support as he deemed fit. A strong man might have used the power thus placed in his hands with potent effect upon the welfare of the country, but unhappily there is no instance of a *cadi* who has done so. Like all other officials of the Turkish Empire, their tenure of office was always uncertain, and, from the worldly point of view, the one and only wise course for them to pursue was to be, in politics and all things outside their strict duty as interpreters and administrators of the law, as absolutely quiescent as might be.

This was the conception that the man who held this post in Bonaparte's time had adopted. Had he been a strong man, a man with some thought of duty and of right, with some desire to benefit the people, he might have accomplished much good. As it was, his influence was mostly that of inaction, that coming from his not-doing rather than from his doing. And he was a man loving his own comfort and most anxious to get through life safely and with the least care, trouble, or vexation of any kind. Of the French he stood in most unwholesome fear, and, while execrating them and all their ways with the most intense hatred, was studiously careful to tender them nothing but the most courteous and affable submission.

In short, he was a miserable, time-serving poltroon, thinking of nothing but his own most worthless self and the peril to his peace of mind, and possibly also to his bodily comfort, that any real or apparent connivance with hostility to the French might bring upon him from the hands of these enemies of God and man, as he esteemed them. So, closing his doors, he listened with trembling ears to the stones crashing through his windows, in deadly fear that the mob would break in and wreak their anger on himself. For some reason, however, the mob were content with the smashing of the windows, which having been done to its satisfaction, surging and shouting it turned about and took a new direction.

Before we follow the crowd it is as well that I should note how clearly this little incident vindicates the people from the charge of slavish servility so often and unjustly brought against them. Let the reader recall what I have said of the power and influence of the *ulema* and of the *cadi*, and that to rebel against the *cadi* was, in the eyes of the people, almost the same thing as to rebel against the *sultan* himself, and thus a crime that brought them perilously close to infidelity, being, in fact, little short of rebellion against heaven itself, yet—strange symptom of servility and curious evidence of the bigotry that is supposed to dominate this people—the shower of stones went smashing through the *cadi's* windows as vigorously and as recklessly as though the mob were in London and the *cadi* an unpopular statesman!

There is another point to be noted as to this incident that may help us to understand the people, and that point is the reason why the people thus fiercely testified their anger. As to this there is no doubt. The reason was plain enough, though not perhaps obvious to the European unfamiliar with Islam and the East.

It was well known that the *cadi* stood in fear of the French, and that he was inclined to temporise and be somewhat too friendly in his relations with them, and much too willing to promote their views and aims; but all these were matters which, while they rendered him the subject of jest and ridicule, were very far from destroying his authority and were quite insufficient to produce the smashing of his windows, for the Egyptians, though lax themselves in obeying the duties and obligations of their religion, and often enough, like others, willing to "*Compound for sins they are inclin'd to, by damning those they have no mind to,*" yet are not given to "*prove their doctrine orthodox by apostolic blows and knocks,*" unless indeed they be urged thereto by some other and more pressing inducement, and would never carry their condemnation of such irregularities to the extent of breaking the windows of the offenders.

It was not, therefore, the *cadi's* alleged unorthodox submission to French influence that the Cairenes so forcibly reprimanded, but what in their eyes was a much more serious fault, that shutting his doors in their faces he should refuse to hear their complaint—this was his offence. I have pointed out before that, in Egypt as elsewhere in the East, the worst of tyrants, as a rule, poses from time to time as a benefactor of the people, and it is rare indeed to find an instance of their openly closing their ears to the cry of the distressed or the plaint of the suffering. They would hear and reject the pleas offered to them, but they would at least hear them.

That the *cadi* should have done this, that he should have listened to what the people had to say, and that having done so he should have refused point-blank to act or speak for them, nay, that he should have roundly abused them and told them to submit—all this they would have borne, though it were with murmuring, grumbling, and unwilling patience and obedience—but that he should refuse to hear them—that they would not bear and would not forgive. That was an abdication of his right to their submission and obedience. And since he would not give them an opportunity of saying by word of mouth what they had to say, they let him know their opinion of his conduct by the very audible and self-interpreting voice of the stones whistling through his windows—a voice admitting of no ambiguity as to the purport of its message.

Looking at the records of window-breakings in Europe and comparing those with this particular breakage, the incident seems but a small one, scarcely worth chronicling, yet, like the battle of the Pyramids, it is noticeable for the consequence that followed it, for it was the poltroonery of the *cadi* and his desire to avoid any personal conflict with the French that decided the issue of the day and turned the mob into the very path the *cadi* would have diverted them from. It was, in fact, upon his reception of the mob that the question of peace or war depended.

No one knew that it was to be so, but, as we shall see, it was the *cadi's* refusal to hear the people that led to the bursting of the storm that had been so long gathering. Had the *cadi* received the people, had he reasoned with them, warned them of the evils that might come from any rashness, or had he taken a higher and bolder position and ordered them to accept the new decree and not to attempt to oppose the French without the sanction of himself and the rest of the *ulema*—had he adopted either of these courses he would have stayed the evil that was at hand, at least for the time. Let us follow the mob and see what happened as it moved away from the *cadi's*.

Rumours of excitement in the town having reached the French headquarters, General Dupuy took a small party of troops and set out to see what was the matter. He had not far to go, and as fate would have it, had scarcely entered the town when he met the angry mob returning from the *cadi's* with no very definite idea as to what it should do next. All doubts they had on this point were set at rest by the appearance of the general. At once the cry went up, "Death to the French!" And with the words went acts. The mob vastly outnumbering the little party of troops with the general and taking them by surprise routed them before they could do much more than assume a posture of defence. In the hurry-scurry of this impromptu battle, one of the first to fall was the gallant general, who was fatally wounded in the neck by one of the primitive weapons with which many of the people were armed—a knife lashed to the end of a long staff. Thus the first result of the *cadi's* cowardly action was the committal of the people to overt rebellion, and the sacrifice of a brave and gallant gentleman to the fury of an angry mob.

Meanwhile in other parts of the town other parties of the people had assembled and were apparently acting quite independently. The firing in the fight between General Dupuy's men and the rebels, as we may now term them, quickly informed the whole town of what was happening, and, the news that a French general had been slain and the troops with him driven off spreading rapidly, practically the whole town rose to arms to follow up this, as they thought it, most auspicious opening of a campaign. At once the gates of the town were seized, the *mustabas*, or stone-built benches in front of the shops torn up to find material for the barricading of the streets, and the people set themselves with a will to prepare for a stubborn fight, little realising the long odds against them.

The house of General Cafarelli in the Birket el Fil quarter of the town, formerly the residence of one of the *beys*, with ample gardens and spacious courtyards surrounded by luxurious apartments, was attacked, and some of the French who happened to be there were struck down before they had time to realise what was taking place. The general himself was absent, as well as several others of the French staff who had their quarters in the roomy buildings of the old *bey's* palace, and the few persons left managing to escape, the mob spent its energies in smashing a valuable collection of scientific instruments and engineering appliances.

Elsewhere in the town Frenchmen and native Christians, wandering about as usual, quite unsuspicious of the danger they were incurring, were ruthlessly cut down, and while the bulk of the rioters were busy preparing to defend the town against the French, some of the lower classes set themselves to pillage the houses of the Christians, but in their anxiety for booty did not stop to spare the houses of Moslems dwelling in the Christian quarters.

Entirely unprepared for the outbreak, it was some little time before the French troops appeared upon the scene, and then they approached the town just where it was defended by the barricades the defence of which had been allotted to the Maghrabins, or Arabs from the Barbary States resident in Cairo, a much more warlike and combative people than the Egyptians. These, attacked by the French, returned the fire of their assailants with such good effect that the French had to retire. Firing was, however, kept up on both sides all through the night with considerable loss to both parties. When morning broke the French found themselves favoured by several circumstances.

Only a part of the town had been able to join in the revolt. The people of Boulac and of Old Cairo, as well as those of the Esbekieh and other quarters in which the French were established in force, being quite unable to offer their townsmen any assistance, and the quarters in revolt being thus those in which there were few, if any, French residents, the French were able to bring up their artillery and concentrate its fire upon the rebels.

So as the day went on the unequal fight proceeded, and under the storm of ball and shot by which they were assailed the Cairenes showed none of the cowardice or distrust of themselves that their critics would have us believe to be among their characteristics. They were on that day a people showing very different traits to those that the great panic at the first triumph of the French had seemed to stamp them with. All through the night and the following day these people, scantily provided with arms and patched-up weapons, stood holding their barricades against the foe that but a few weeks before had scattered what they had regarded as the invincible army of the Mamaluks. Truly a stubborn, stiff-necked people when they took it into their heads to be so—a people who, notwithstanding their everyday docility, could give their rulers no little trouble whenever they had a mind to do so.

Midday passed, and the battle went on with no abatement of ardour on either side, and with no talk or thought of submission on the side of the rebels. But as the time of the afternoon prayer approached the *ulema* who could, in spite of their pacific character, form a better and more reliable estimate of the probable final result of the struggle, appealed to the people, and went to General Bonaparte himself to intercede for peace, begging him to stop the bombardment that was making such havoc in the town, and was more harmful to the innocent and helpless than to those most in fault. Bonaparte, accusing the *ulema* of being responsible for the outbreak, reproached them bitterly, but finally yielded to their entreaties, and, ordering the batteries to be silenced, promised an amnesty for all who should at once lay down their arms.

Evening was drawing near as the *sheikhs* returned from their self-appointed embassy. The people, wearied with the heavy strain of the long night and day of constant action, with their small stock of munitions almost exhausted, and finding their strength failing, with their women and children shrieking and weeping in terror at the houses crumbling around them under the hail of shell from the French batteries, were compelled to accept the offered peace, and as the sun went down the firing on both sides stopped, save that the warlike Maghrabins, who thoroughly enjoyed the battle, kept up a fight upon their own account for yet an hour or so longer, being most loath to abandon it at all.

The storm that thus ended almost as abruptly as it had broken out had cost the French one of their best generals, and not a few valuable lives of less degree in the service. The Egyptians, too, had lost heavily. Many peaceful citizens had been slain, and many houses more or less completely wrecked. For the Cairenes it had been their "baptism of fire." They had taken up arms to fight, scarcely knowing how to handle them, and to be under the fire of an enemy was a wholly new experience to them, scarce one of them having even seen a cannon fired save for the harmless purpose of a salute. Yet, astounded as they were at the destruction wrought by the French guns, they had held their ground staunchly all through that to them most terrible day, and in doing so learned something of their own strength though almost nothing of how to use it.

But whatever the people had learned, Bonaparte learned but little from the storm. It taught him, indeed, that the people were not quite so docile as he had thought them to be, and that they were still less friendly to the French and their ideas than he had imagined possible; but that was all. It taught him nothing of that which it would have been most serviceable for him to have learned—something of the real nature of the people and of the best and wisest way of dealing with them. Had he been a great man in any true sense of the phrase, had he been even a clever one, or still less nobly, even a cunning one, he might have turned the storm and its collapse very greatly indeed to his own advantage.

Never from the day of his arrival had he had the people so completely at his mercy, so wholly under his own control, if he had only known how to exercise it. But knowing no means of attaining his objects but through the brute force of his battalions and such terror as they could inspire, and no higher diplomacy than the yielding of minor points as to which he was in truth indifferent, he, most naturally for him, did exactly the things most calculated to strengthen the hatred of the people for the French, and thus to heap up difficulties in his own path.

Whether done through thoughtless indifference or from a wanton desire to outrage the feelings of the people, the French cavalry were stabled in the mosque of the Azhar, the great university, not only of Egypt but of the whole Moslem world, and this venerated building, to which students came from every land in which Islam had even a small group of followers, was desecrated and defiled, as well by the horses of the troops as by the troopers themselves, in every possible way. If it had been the object of the French to humiliate and insult the people and their faith in the greatest conceivable degree, this was of all others the surest and simplest way of accomplishing it.

Once more the *ulema* went to Bonaparte to plead with him for the exercise of a little humanity, and once more he ungraciously granted their request. The evacuation of the mosque was ordered, but, as always, the concession was marred, so far as Bonaparte could mar it, by the arrest of a number of the *sheikhs* accused of having fomented or encouraged the revolt, and by his refusal to hear any intercession on their behalf.

The storm had come and gone. Like all storms it had left a trail of damage, but it had to some extent cleared the air. Frenchmen and Egyptians understood one another less than before and yet better; and so drawing daily more and more apart, both literally and figuratively, the French—many of whom had been living here and there in the town amidst the people—began to move and gather themselves more and more together, whilst the Egyptians living in the Esbekieh and other parts that had been specially adopted by the French were ordered to leave.

Other changes followed. The flood-tide of reforms had reached its height and ceased to flow, to the vast relief of the people no longer driven hither and thither by its currents and eddies. The *sheikhs* accused of fomenting sedition having been executed, the daily stream of arrests and executions that had continued throughout the occupation was checked, and so the people sadly, but not sullenly, settled themselves down peacefully enough to wait the early coming of the Turkish army that, as they fondly believed, was to scatter the French as the *sirocco* scatters the sand-heaps of the desert, so that the place should know them no more, and their very name be but as the memory of a dream.

Yet with all this, while the people had just cause to congratulate themselves that their outbreak was not altogether unfruitful in its effects, and to grieve over the long list of their dead and wounded and the crumbled ruins of their dwellings, the truth is that they were repenting for their wild outburst; for now that the passionate wrath that had urged them on was gone, the philosophy that had carried them through so many centuries of woe reproached them for their faithlessness. They had fought a stout fight against long odds, and though beaten in form had proved victorious in substance, since, as I have said, the torrent of reform that had so exasperated them was stayed, and it was the French and not they who had to abandon in every way the position they had occupied. But as reflection came they asked themselves whether the gain was worth the cost, and finding less cause for exultation than for regret, so far from rejoicing over what they had done, spoke only of the fight to ask God's forgiveness for their madness.

But the French, knowing nothing of the true feelings of the people, and quite unable to fathom their thoughts, so far from thinking that they had never before been so safe from the anger of the people, began to take all sorts of needless precautions, and not only kept together in their walks and wanderings, but carried arms and shunned the native quarters of the town.

CHAPTER 11

After the Storm

Under the changed conditions in which the French were now living they began to find time hanging heavily on their hands, so they turned their attention to the task of providing occupation for their leisure hours, and as a first step in the realisation of this desirable object built themselves an assembly-room. This and some other projects kept them busy for some weeks, and helped to heal the bitterness that the revolt had created, and, like the Egyptians, if not ready to bury the past altogether, they were willing enough to let it lie in oblivion, and, largely influenced by the fact that the destruction of the fleet had left them locked in the country with no very hopeful possibility of their being soon able to receive help from France, they set themselves to get on with the people as well as might be, and included in their schemes some intended at once to please and gratify the Cairenes and impress them with a sense of the superiority of the French.

Among the other devices that it was thought could not fail to serve these ends and win general applause was the construction of a Montgolfier balloon. This having been successfully accomplished, the public were invited to come and see a wonderful contrivance by which the French were able to communicate with far-off lands, and thus, if need should arise, seek and obtain help from their native country or elsewhere. Such an announcement naturally brought the Egyptians, who are always curious to see and inspect novelties of all kinds, in crowds to the Esbekieh on the day appointed for the ascent.

Fortune, however, was not generous to the French, and though the balloon was a success in all things that skill could command, an adverse and indifferent wind left it loitering in sight until the moment of its collapse arrived, and it sank ignominiously to earth, to the great scorn of the people, who derisively styled it a "big kite," and compared it to the kites that the boys of Egypt had long been wont to amuse themselves with. The failure was a sad blow to the French, who had hoped to see the balloon float majestically away and disappear in the north, as though it were indeed bound for Paris.

A worthier and more successful enterprise that the French engaged in was the opening of a public library in the district to the south of the town still known as the Nasrieh. Of this Gabarty, who is not sparing in his ridicule of the balloon, gives an enthusiastic description, and records with the most unstinted appreciation his sense of the high courtesy with which the French received all visitors. He himself went often, and tells us not only of the delight with which he enjoyed its wonders, but of the pleasure afforded by the welcome offered to all visitors, and especially to those who showed an interest in or knowledge of the sciences.

For their inspection all the treasures of the place were freely produced, and all help given them to understand the object and worth of what they were shown. There were many things in the library that the Egyptian visitors could thoroughly appreciate—rare Oriental manuscripts, maps and atlases of all parts of the world, illustrated volumes, astronomical and other scientific diagrams and philological works. For all these, as well as for the French savants who so freely and liberally put their time and knowledge at the service of their guests, Gabarty has unstinted praise and admiration.

Even more successful than the library, from the popular point of view, was the laboratory that the French threw open to all comers. Popular science was then in its infancy. The chemistry of today was altogether unknown and undreamt of. Electricity was in its early babyhood, even the telegraph being yet to come. Steam was an unharnessed giant. Gas, photography, and a host of things that are now-a-days among the most commonplace of our surroundings were unknown, not only in Egypt but in Europe. And by the Nile, where art and science once flourished, the little knowledge that still survived was the inheritance and privilege of the *ulema*, and was sadly cramped and debased by the false theology that had elevated religious pedantry above all other knowledge or desire.

It is no wonder, therefore, that the French were able to astonish their guests beyond measure by showing them a host of those "experiments in natural science" that in our own boyhood days we delighted in when presented to us as the "magic of chemistry," such as the production of a solid by the mixing of two liquids. The marvels of electricity as then known were also displayed, and, as Gabarty says with his customary candour, "other wonders that intelligence like ours could neither understand nor explain."

All the visitors to the library and laboratory were not, of course, as intelligent or appreciative as the Sheikh Gabarty, and some of the few historians who condescend to mention things unconnected with the battles and bloodshed that is their proper subject, record with glee, as a fitting illustration of the native mind, the story of the *sheikh* who, having beheld with Oriental stolidity all the marvels the French could show him, asked whether the science of Europe was equal to the task of enabling him to be present in two places at once, and, being assured that it could not, expressed his contempt for such lamentably imperfect science. That the incident really occurred there is no reason to doubt, but the *sheikh's* attitude was not such a childishly absurd one as our friends the historians would wish us to believe.

To understand it we must go back to the time and the place, though even from the present we may gain a hint. Not long since an Italian boy showed me a little booklet that had been given to him by his teacher, a Catholic priest. It was a short history of the life of a saint, and recorded how a mule had gone on its knees out of respect for the "Host." The book had the printed imprimatur of his Holiness the late Pope. I asked the boy if he really believed the story, and he replied, "Why not?" Why not, indeed! Luther not only believed in the devil, but saw him, and threw his ink-bottle at him; notwithstanding which, I, though not a Christian in any sense, most firmly believe in Luther, and hold him as one far beyond the world's great hero Bonaparte in all that constitutes true greatness.

I can, therefore, quite understand how a pious *sheikh* in Cairo, in the year of grace 1799, could believe in the possibility of a man being, by the aid of lawful or unlawful arts and sciences, both here and there at the same time, for to him, as to Luther, belief in the supernatural made all things possible, and, just as Luther had a hundred hearsay traditions of the pious and godly to justify his interpretation of the hallucination produced by an overworked brain, so the *sheikh* had not only traditions but the sworn testimony of many eyewitnesses to the possibility of the impossibility in which he thus expressed his belief. And as it held in the closing days of the eighteenth century, so in these, the early years of the twentieth, the Church of Rome still holds as heretic whoever disputes the truth of the worshipping mule, and in the East not only are miracles firmly believed in, but do actually, in a sense, take place. A night's march from Hodeidah, up in the hills of Yemen, there was in the seventies of the last century a certain saint who held open court for all who came, and it was the tradition, and, as I can testify, the verity of the place that when his guests sat down to meals the more they ate the more was left. I have seen this miracle as it was, and perhaps still is, commonly accounted, repeated not once, but again and again during my stay.

And this same saint was held by all the populace of Hodeidah, which in those days did not number a single Christian among its residents, to have on many occasions attended the public prayers in Hodeidah and those in Sana'a at one and the same time. The saint, grown old and bedridden when I saw him, was a fine old Arab, and though speaking with difficulty, asked me a few intelligent questions about India and England. Whence, as it seems to me, having abundance of such evidence before him, and having a boundless faith in the omnipotence of the Creator and of His regard for the doings of His people, the mocking *sheikh* in the French laboratory was in fact ridiculing not French science but French infidelity. In the Cairo of today there are but few who have such simple, honest faith as that old *sheikh*. Whether on the whole Cairo or its people are much the better of the change is a question not altogether so beyond discussion as my reader probably thinks.

But whether the old *sheikh* was serious or ironical in his question, it is quite certain that the Sheikh Gabarty was perfectly serious in his comments, and in the records of these things that he has left us there is much to guide us in forming an idea of the Egyptian of the period, for though he was one of the "learned," he was essentially one of the people, and, like them, when under no special restraint, accustomed to speak his mind clearly and without any other bias than the impulse of the moment. Born in Cairo in the year 1754, he was like Sayed Mahomed Kerim, the Governor of Alexandria, of Arab origin, and, like him, though preserving much of the Arab in his nature, essentially an Egyptian. Originally from Zeilah on the African coast of the Gulf of Aden, his family had been settled in Egypt for seven generations, and had taken the name Jibarty, or, as it is pronounced in Egypt, Gabarty, from their first home, Jibart being one of the names by which Zeilah is still known.

Claiming descent from the family of Abou Talib, that uncle of the Prophet of Islam who, though unconverted to the faith of his nephew, accorded him his protection and sympathy in the days when he so sorely needed a friend, the Gabarty family had in Egypt been scarcely less famous for its origin than for its piety, learning, and wealth. Sheikh Ali, the great-grandfather of the Sheikh Abdu Rahman Gabarty—the historian of whom I am writing—attained full honours as a saint, and in the time of Bonaparte his tomb at Edfoo was still a place of pilgrimage for the pious, not only of Egypt, but of Arabia and Abyssinia and other lands of Islam.

Another notable member of the family was the Sheikh Abdu Rahman's father, a man of great learning, a deeply read student of all the sciences and branches of learning then cultivated in Egypt, a noted bibliophile and the author of many works covering a wide range of subjects. The "Standard-bearer of knowledge" and "Moon of Islam and its followers" are some of the phrases in which his son with filial piety describes him, and it is certain that, considering his time and place, he was not unworthy of them. Recognised by the *ulema* as the most accomplished and brilliant scholar of the day, in private life he was beloved for his affability, generosity, and public spirit, the latter being evidenced by, among other things, his establishing in his own house a lending library, which he placed at the free disposal of all students.

As an author he produced a long list of works chiefly of a controversial character, but some of an eminently practical nature, such as his guide to the ceremonies of the pilgrimage to Mecca. Nor was he without inventive skill—an instrument for ascertaining the *kibla*, or point to which all Moslems are bound to turn when praying, and a circular calendar covering a long period of time, and supplying corresponding dates for a number of different eras, such as the Moslem, Coptic and Greek, being among the more noteworthy. He was also a great amateur of sundials, and constructed many of various types. His scientific knowledge, public spirit, and practical nature were all combined to enable him to carry out single-handed a reform in the weights and measures of the Cairo markets.

Abdu Rahman, the historian, was a worthy son of this distinguished man. Like him, a great scholar, though less broad in his reading, an acute thinker, indefatigable worker, an earnest and conscientious follower of his religion, and yet free, as his history proves, of all fanaticism and bigotry, independent in spirit, truthful and candid in speech and writing, yet withal courteous and generous in his intercourse with others, it was but natural that he should succeed his father as one of the foremost of the *sheikhs* of the Azhar University, and that he should have been one of the men chosen to form the *dewan* when Bonaparte asked for the names of the leading men.

Such being the man and his origin, it is not difficult to understand how bitter to him must have been the events that had followed the arrival of the French. But he records the history of the time with the staid reserve of the "Father of History," setting down the good and the bad with equal fidelity, neither concealing the truth as he saw it, nor speaking aught in malice. All through his story of the French occupation one can see how greatly his heart rebelled against it, but, none the less, he never grudges the invaders his admiration when they could win it, as in the case of the library and the laboratory, though he could, when he would, be sarcastic enough, as when laughing at the fiasco of the balloon, and is capable of righteous indignation, not only against the French but also against the Moslems who sinned against that which he held to be the laws of right and truth.

So while he more than hints his belief that many of the "reforms" were but excuses for the collection of taxes, he readily admits the utility of the registration of births, marriages, and deaths, sees no harm in the wearing of the cockade, and admits the benefits of disinfection and quarantine. His book is therefore what he never intended it to be—a wonderful picture of the man himself as well as it is that which he intended it to be—a full and, above all else, a truthful account of the events of his time. And it is even more than this, for it is to those who know something of the East and its peoples a valuable guide to the character of the Egyptians, and, without any intention on his part, or indeed any idea that he is touching such a subject, he is constantly showing us how and why the French failed to gain the goodwill or friendship of the people.

And through it all, in the gathering of the storm as in its burst, and in the days of dire grief that followed it, we see the man himself placid and calm, with unfaltering though aching heart, going steadily on, maintaining his daily life as much as might be unchanged, ever in fear and yet never in fear; ever in fear that the morrow might bring some new trouble or vexation, never in fear but that, come what might, in the end all must be well, for after all was not all this flood of affliction let loose on the country "that God might accomplish His decrees"?

And as Gabarty thought of all these things, so, in a measure, thought all the Egyptians. Much as they enjoy peace, comfort, society, and all the good things of this life, they all sit in the tub of Diogenes and mock at the power and grandeur of the great. Robert of Sicily in his magnificent attire may be a very gorgeous spectacle, but they are quite prepared to see him tomorrow, or the day after, running "bare-headed and besprent with mire," and so when Bonaparte, who, not having yet heard the dismal droning of St. Helena's surges, by no means shared such silly ideas, issued his decrees and warned the people of the certain destruction that was to overtake all who dared oppose him, they, though they held their tongues, felt inclined to reply, as did Akhbar the Great of India's prisoner, "Would it not be well to say 'With God's permission'?" And of what avail all this bloodshed and rapine? What madness and utter folly all this tumultuous turbulence of *beys* and Bonapartes! What could they gain by it? Did they forget "th' inevitable hour?" Were there no graves awaiting them wherein they would lie and rot while others no wiser than they would be furiously fighting over the heritage they had left?

And so also for smaller things. Why worry and fret about these reforms? They may be good and beneficial in their way, but peace and quiet were better. And if the French really desired reforms, why not give the people the reforms they did really long for? To live in peace and quiet and be left to seek their own welfare in their own manner? These were things to be sought after and, if possible, attained: things worth some little sacrifice. Give them these and leave them free to enjoy their lives as they would, and they would pay willingly enough whatever reasonable taxes you might desire, even though these pressed a little heavily upon them.

And these being the ideals of the Egyptians, it should be easy for the reader to see that after all for them the French, as rulers of the land, were scarcely as desirable as the *beys*. Instead of giving the people liberty, this was just what they took from them. Under the French they felt all the horror that convicts have told us they have felt in English and other jails at the knowledge that they were always under restraint and observation. The French complained that the Egyptians were ungrateful, but it is not easy for a man to be grateful for a benefit of which he is unconscious. That the French were in many things their superiors the Egyptians could plainly see; that they were far beyond them in the arts and sciences and manufactures; that their ideas of governing and administering the town and country were better than those of the Turks, or Mamaluks: all these were things that the Egyptians could and did admit, but they could not and would not admit that the benefit to be derived from these was worth anything like the price the French asked them to pay.

From the days of the Pharaohs they had carried their bricks and their mortar in hods on their heads or on their shoulders. The French wheelbarrows were ingenious and useful things, and there was no reason why the Egyptians should not avail themselves of these or any other of the endless conveniences that they were now seeing for the first time, provided that the employment of these things was not to be made a burden, and that they were employed to lighten and not to increase the labourer's task. And it was so in higher things and among the higher classes. It was good to register births and deaths—was it not the custom of the Arabs themselves from the very earliest days?— but it was not good to tie people down to making their records in a certain way, at a certain time, at a certain place, or to put them under pains and penalties for any failure in conforming to the burthensome rules the French had laid down with respect to such matters.

It was thus that Gabarty and his countrymen reasoned then and it is thus that the Egyptian still reasons, and while they so reasoned and so reason it was and is impossible for the European and the Egyptian to coalesce socially or politically. The ultimate aim of the French and of the Egyptians was one and the same thing—the happiness of the people; but their conceptions of happiness were radically distinct, nor were their ideas as to the means whereby happiness was to be attained less irreconcilable. Throughout the world, turn where we will, we find all men engaged in the same pursuit, carrying on the same struggle.

The silly-pated fools lounging at the bars of London and the hard-handed labourer toiling at his daily work, the Salvation Army lass tending the sick and poor, and the Buddhist fanatic burning himself alive—these and the million types that range between these extremes, these are all seeking the same goal, struggling each in his or her own way for the attainment of the same end, the realisation of their own ideal of happiness. I have in an earlier chapter tried to show why the Egyptian and the English characters are of necessity so different, and in doing that I have, to some extent at least, shown why the French and the Egyptians were so opposed in their valuation of the reforms that Bonaparte was so assiduous in introducing.

That Bonaparte cared the value of a brass farthing for the welfare of Egypt or the happiness of the Egyptians is simply inconceivable, but that he really and earnestly desired to see both these things re-alised is certain. Had an overwhelming inundation swept Egypt and the Egyptians into the sea, Bonaparte's chief regret would have been that he had neither ships nor men with which to avail himself of this new and most convenient route to India. But so long as their exist-ence was conducive, or might possibly be made conducive, to his own interests he certainly desired that the country should prosper, that he might reap the benefit, and that the people should be happy, or at least content, so that he need not waste his resources in combating or providing against hostility on their part. This is the debt, and this only, that Egypt owes to the goodwill of Bonaparte.

In Gabarty's picture of the library and laboratory we find French-men of a very different type to the Corsican. To these men and to oth-ers that were yet to come Egypt owes much. Had there been nothing to counteract their influence Egypt would indeed have had reason to bless the day the French arrived, for their patient, courteous, kindly enthusiasm was just what was needed to give the people a real and lasting impulse towards better things, and as we see the pettiness and mean ambitions of Bonaparte for ever blocking this the only true road to the ends he desired, we cannot but feel that, once in the country, the best thing he ever did for it was to take himself out of it as he did, stealing away like a thief in the night, deserting the army that had served him faithfully and well utterly reckless of the fate that might await them. That, indeed, was good for Egypt.

But the Frenchmen who would and could have benefited the country had many difficulties to overcome; had they once been in a position to set themselves seriously to the task, they would have wrought much good. But they were forced to act as if the happiness of Egypt was to be attained by casting its social and political conditions in the mould of the French Republic. To the Egyptian, not yet being able to fully comprehend the spirit of these men, and seeing nothing in the French occupation but the worries and vexations with which the tyranny of Bonaparte overwhelmed them, the only happiness the French could offer them was to leave them alone. Their ideals and the French were altogether different and never could agree.

The Egyptian could see this but the French could not, and least of all Bonaparte. What was possible was that the Egyptians should learn much and benefit much from French civilisation and its adaptation to the needs and circumstances of the country and its people. This and nothing more. But Bonaparte was of all men the least capable of seeing such a fact as this, and so he kept stretching the Egyptians on a Procrustean bed of reform, and was wroth that they did not enjoy the experience.

Yet in the daily life of the people around him, if he could but have seen it as it was, and not simply as it appeared to him to be, there were ample facts to guide him in the framing of a policy that might have attracted and so gained, as far as was possible for him to gain it, the goodwill of the population. Scattered here and there, in and out of the city, were the ruined palaces and mouldering mosques of the *caliphs* and *sultans* of the past, and of the builders the people knew little more than their names, if so much, and there were tombs of men, often of the humblest rank, to which the passer-by turned for a moment to pray with that indifference to the true teaching of his religion and boundless faith in his own superstitions that is characteristic of the lower classes in the country.

A most significant fact this survival of the unfittest, for in truth this is the right adjective to apply to most of these saints of great popularity in Egypt. There were indeed among these, men, like the Sheikh Gabarty of whom I have spoken, who were not unworthy of reverent remembrance, but these would have been the first to forbid the use of prayers to, instead of those for, the dead. But the Egyptian, like most men, needs a hero to worship in some form or other, and since he could not by any possible stretch of the imagination bring himself to look upon the *caliphs* and *sultans* and *beys* of the past who should have abundantly supplied his need as worthy of his reverence, he was in a measure compelled to accept such paltry makeshift heroes as his "saints."

These he endowed with all the virtues that he would have fain seen the living rulers of the land practise, and adding an abundance of miracles to their credit, treated them as the heathen of old did, and as the Hindoos of today still do their gods and goddesses, exalted them into guardian deities for the locality in which they had lived or were buried. Folly and superstition, and, for the Moslem, rank heresy and infidelity, yet most significant and instructive for those who would understand the people thus wandering from the right way. Most significant, for after all people, however "stupid" and "silly," do not wander without some reason, without some object to attract them.

Bonaparte could not understand this, and not only could he not understand it, but he did precisely the same thing himself in dealing with the people. Like Mr. Worldly-wise-man, he and they were content to do as other people did without troubling to consider whether there were not a better way to be found. As for the people, they enjoyed their bypath as Christian did his—until he awoke to find himself in the clutches of Giant Despair; but Bonaparte could get no further than to wonder at the wholly unprofitable roughness of the path he had chosen, and the utter unwillingness of the people to cross the stile and follow his way.

Had he stopped to ask what were the chief virtues with which the people endowed their heroes, he would have found that first, and so far first that all the rest came lagging almost out of sight, was that wondrous virtue so esteemed throughout all the East, and to which the Catholic Church lends its applauding patronage—utter contempt and indifference to the things of this world. The naked imbecile wandering among the tombs is to the Eastern not a "man possessed with a devil," but "el Mubarik." *El Mubarik!* The Blessed! The man whom God has blessed by freeing his mind from all the cares and worries of this life. Astounding ignorance! Degrading superstition! That, my dear reader, is no doubt how you see it. That is how Bonaparte saw it, and, it may surprise you to hear, that is how Gabarty the historian saw it.

And I will follow such high authorities so far as to admit that seeing such things as you do and they did, only "darkly and as through a glass," your view is a very correct one. But if the people thus err, there is a reason—a reason that you will never discover so long as you wrap yourself up in your superior intelligence, and will not stoop to learn from the facts you so glibly criticise. Not that the solution of this mystery is either recondite or difficult of attainment.

Far from that. If I could present to your inspection two maps of the world, one whereon was marked by varying depths of colour those parts of the world wherein the bulk of the people find life most burthensome and least attractive, and the other marked in the same way and in the same colours to show where this reverence for the imbecile and other kindred follies are most rife, you would say, "But the two maps are the same!" and you would be correct, for this "lowest of all superstitions" is but the expression of the hopeless, helpless longing for freedom from care that comes to those whose lives are one long burthen, unaided and unrelieved by strength of mind or healthy training. Of what use to appeal to such with the arguments that might stir the blood and stimulate the thoughts of the Frenchman, be he *chatelain* or *sans culotte*? Surely so long as Bonaparte and the French could not see these things, neither he nor they could do much to lift or elevate the people or to render their lives happy!

Nor if the lower classes were thus effectually shut out from French influence were the better informed much less widely separated from them. Children fighting for garden plots and brass-headed nails!

Ruskin might have written that parable to illustrate the aspect which French ambitions offered to the *ulema*. Garden plots and brass-headed nails! Things useful and desirable in themselves, but not worth fighting for. "Vanity of vanities, all is vanity!" that is forever the song of the *ulema*, and though with Pope they hold that "Not a vanity is given in vain," yet they will not admit that any given vanity is worth fighting for. They are ready enough to turn aside in Vanity Fair and to enjoy its vanities, but they never forget that they are vanities.

As the old Arabic has it, "*This world is a place of going, not a place of staying.*" Why, then, toil and moil for mere vanities that we must leave behind us? If we labour at all let it be for treasures, not vanities—treasures that once they are ours are ours for all time and all eternity, treasures that all the armies of all the Bonapartes and *sultans* and *beys* in the world cannot rob us of—deeds of charity and deeds of piety, kindly words and kindly acts, mercy and forgiveness.

This is the philosophy of the Egyptian and of the Eastern, as it is that of Christ Himself. "*Thou shalt love the Lord thy God and thy neighbour as thyself.*" Christian clergymen of all denominations teach it and preach it, Christian citizens profess it, Christian civilisation applauds—and ignores it. That most insignificant-looking of letters, the Greek *iota*, was sufficient to split the Christian Church in twain, but this philosophy has never caused a breath or whisper of dissent or discord. The Christian priest, the Moslem Sheikh, the Brahman Guru, the Buddhist Lama, all are agreed in this, in the dogma, though not all in its application. The Eastern takes it very literally.

The European looks upon it as a pretty ideal, good to be spoken of now and then, but having nothing whatever to do with the realities of actual life. Whence Plugson of Undershot, whom Carlyle places on a level with the Chactaw Indians, with, as I think, scant justice to the Chactaw, whose ideal is, or rather was, a higher one that Plugson's, seeing that Plugson has no higher ideal than his own individual interests, whereas the Chactaw always had the honour of his tribe in mind, and would, if need be, die for that very unsubstantial figment, whence it is evident that the Chactaw had in reality advanced towards the highest real civilisation a full stage further than has Plugson. For all true civilisation is, in spite of certain philosophers' opinions, the negation of individualism.

The very lowest type of humanity is the man thinking, acting only for himself, like the brutes of the forest, knowing no ambition, no need, beyond his own individual wants or wishes. Such men as these are only possible in a "highly civilised" community, and will be found most abundantly in the most civilised and among the highest, or at least the wealthiest classes of these. Among mere savages, by a merciful provision of nature, such men wage such ruthless war with each other that it is well-nigh impossible for two to survive. But if these men exist in and are a product of civilisation, it is only as the scum floating on the surface of the molten metal, as base, as mean, and worthless as the dregs that lie at its bottom.

As to the Egyptian, neither a Plugson nor yet a Chactaw, he is rather to be compared to poor old Abbot Hugo, or some of his patient, faithful monks, striving in a certain halting, faltering, wholly incompetent, and yet withal more or less earnest way to do right— very prone, like Christian himself, to be tempted over the stile into the pleasant-looking byways of the road, and to start back at the sight of the lions at Mr. Interpreter's house, and yet, like Faithful, resolute enough to stand unabashed in the pillories of Vanity Fair and to face undaunted the terrors of the Valley of the Shadow. How could such men as these fall down and worship the golden calf of the French Republic? How could the French, whose farthest horizon was no further off than the short limits of "the average duration of life," comprehend the Egyptian?

The first brief fraternising of the two peoples had been as the momentary intermixing of water and oil suddenly thrown into a common receptacle; thereafter their inherent mutual repugnance inevitably drove them apart, and in the calm that followed the riot the separation became daily more and more complete. Hence it was that Gabarty and all his kind, while they could admire and wonder at the marvels the French showed them, and could and did appreciate much of the law, order, and good discipline they obeyed, yet, weighing these things in the balance of man's relations to the infinite as they conceived these to be, rejected them.

It is not to be supposed that the Egyptians measured in any such way as I have done the difference between themselves and the French, or that they thought of, or were even aware of, the philosophy by which they were guided. They simply looked upon the French from a very simple, practical, everyday point of view, first as usurping foreigners, and secondly as men with a wholly unaccountable, extraordinary, and irrational conception of life and its needs; a people showing a strange indifference to that oldest and most indisputable of all truths— that man is mortal, and who, giving all their thoughts and energies to vain theories and ambitions, were hopelessly bewildered and befogged by their own cleverness, madly bartering true happiness for a brilliant but worthless imitation; a people the more mad and the more foolish that there was no need for them to make such an unprofitable trade. For in the French conception of civilisation and happiness there was little if anything absolutely irreconcilable with the Egyptian view. There was no reason why men should not profit to the utmost from all the arts, sciences, knowledge, or progress of any kind, but these things should be sought as the complement and completion of better things and not as the ultimate good, and they could be sought much better if the people were not worried by the endless forms and formalities, needless rules and regulations, and idle and burthensome restraints the French put upon them.

This was, and is, the Egyptian's ideal of civilisation—not unlike that of Carlyle and Ruskin: civilisation as a means and not as an end— an ideal of which we at home seem at last to be getting a faint, glimmering perception, as evidenced by the victory of the "living wage" verity over the "supply and demand" falsity—a victory whereby English civilisation has been advanced a long step towards the Egyptian and Islamic ideal for which the rabbit-brained "smart set" and other puerilities and senilities have so much contempt. Unfortunately the Egyptian fails to see the duty that his ideal imposes upon him, and thus only too well justifies the criticisms of those who take the imperfections of the man as those of his ideals. They did not, and they as yet do not, clearly see that however high and noble a man's ideal may be, it is useless and vain unless it be converted into action.

The best of seed kept in a glass case for men to admire is but an unprofitable perfection. That it may be prolific, beneficial to men, it is needful to take it from its case and plant it in the soil to grow. So with our ideals—however perfect, however beautiful, they are worthless unless planted in the soil of that strenuous effort President Roosevelt has so rightly lauded. Perhaps someday, when Englishmen in general begin to see these things more clearly, when we begin to understand that after all the swelling of the budget and the filling of our individual pockets are not the highest, nor indeed high aims at all, when we can openly accept and act upon the creed of Burns, that "the rank is but the guinea's stamp," then perhaps we may be able to help the Egyptian also to a higher and purer conception of true civilisation. At present, not possessing that article, it is scarcely possible for us to transfer it to or share it with the Egyptian or anyone else.

CHAPTER 12

Peace Without Honour

The months succeeding the suppression of the revolt were months of peace though scarcely of honour, and certainly not of content. The people were no longer harassed by daily innovations or angered by daily arrests and executions, and looking forward to the early coming of a Turkish army as certain to sooner or later bring them relief, they submitted passively to the presence of the French. The *dewan*, which had been suspended from the time of the revolt, was at the end of the year re-formed, and Bonaparte took the opportunity to issue a proclamation in which he had the foolish arrogance to claim to be inspired. This, addressed to Mahomedans, was a gross mistake, and is yet another proof of his inability to learn from experience or to comprehend the task he was so blunderingly pursuing.

The Egyptians received the proclamation with the ridicule it deserved, but they were careful to keep their opinion of it to themselves, having learned very thoroughly the exact value of the "liberty, equality, and fraternity" of which they had heard so much, and knew perfectly well that "liberty" must by no means be taken to include the liberty of criticising the French. As to "equality," Bonaparte did certainly show some impartiality—at all events in matters not directly affecting the French. Thus some native Christians, who had been too bold in availing themselves of their new-found liberty to insult the Moslems, were summarily punished, not so much probably for the offence as to discourage their provoking reprisals from which the French might suffer.

Some soldiers too, who had been captured after raiding the house of a Moslem and outraging the women in it, were executed, this being a serious offence against discipline. These matters were referred to by the general in his proclamation as evidence of his friendship for and

130

desire to do justice to the people. But the people put their own construction upon these acts and his allusion to them. The whole tenor of the system under which they were so unwillingly living was, in their opinion, utterly opposed to justice and reason, and they could not bring themselves to conceive these incidents as anything more than mere concessions made to mislead them. They had always been accustomed to receive in their private affairs a certain amount of justice under the *beys*.

This was indeed usually of a very rough and ready kind. Thus one of the *beys* one day passing through the town meeting a citizen who had just bought some meat from a butcher in the market, took it into his head to see whether the seller had given his customer full weight, and finding that he had not done so at once ordered the deficiency to be supplied from the butcher's own body. French justice was less fantastic and impulsive than this, whether it was more effective is not so certain, but it had to the Egyptian mind the great defect of being in general less amenable to the pleadings of mercy, and was, like the *beys'*, so often misdirected as to become injustice. Thus Bonaparte gained but little from his good intentions in this respect.

As to "Fraternity," the cannon of the revolt had been the stormy requiem of all possibility of that. The battered houses of the town were infinitely more eloquent to the people than all that Bonaparte could say, and he could have but little assistance in preaching or enforcing his ideas on this subject, for the French generally, though quite loyal, were scarcely enthusiastic in their efforts to realise his wishes in this direction, and could in any case do but little, while the native Christians who could have done much, unable to rise above the pettiness of their own vindictive feelings, so far from seeking to promote friendship between the French and the Moslems, lost no opportunity of exciting the one against the other. So poor Fraternity lay neglected in the tomb that Bonaparte's blundering had so speedily and so unnecessarily dug for it.

All through the occupation the worst friends that the French had were the Christians of the country. Divided among themselves, they were at one, though not united, in the feelings with which they quickly learned to regard the French. There was no open disunion nor apparent discord, but the bitterness of sectarian animosities that prevailed among them was of the keenest. The Franks being Christians of the "Orthodox" or Greek Church held the Copts as heretics, and these looked upon those as *infidels*. Nor were they less divided by

131

their political and social ideas and habits, and, as such rival sects always are, were more strongly moved by their mutual distrust than by their common Christianity. This, indeed, served them as a bond only for evil in their common hatred for the Moslems. These, though they had for centuries to endure more oppression, injustice, and tyranny than either of the two Christian peoples had ever suffered from, were conscious of and showed a dignity and self-respect that was galling and offensive to the others.

Our friends the historians lose no opportunity of condemning the Moslems for this characteristic, denouncing it as "arrogant pride," "fanatical conceit," and I know not what else. But though the Moslem too often renders himself liable to criticism on this point, his fault in no way abrogates the truth that the self-respect that is in varying degrees the birthright of all men is to him alone justified by his religion, for Islam alone of all religions, while teaching the frailty of man's nature, teaches also the doctrine that man is naturally inclined to good, and that his sins and his follies are the result not of a corrupt nature but of ignorance and false teaching—a nobler and truer conception than the degrading superstition that it is their nature to do evil.

The Moslem, unlike those Methodists whose sole anxiety in life is for the salvation of their own miserable souls, has no salvation to seek. As a Moslem he is assured of eternal happiness. It is inevitable, therefore, that he should respect himself, even as the Christian who has but a jot of belief in the teaching of his religion cannot look upon himself as other than a "child of wrath," by nature evil and a lover of evil. Truly a grovelling, debasing creed. And it is with creeds as with ideals. That they should influence the whole life and nature of a man it is by no means necessary that he should be conscious of their influence, much less that he should analyse or even be capable of analysing it. Whence no degradation, no tyranny, no misery can deprive the Moslem of the self-respect that is his inheritance—a self-respect no other religion permits, and one that no follower of any other religion can by any possibility enjoy, since he who has it must be a believer in the essential doctrines of Islam and thus, though he know it not, a Moslem.

This is an essential difference that must for ever hold all Moslem peoples apart from all others. I have shown already how not the Moslem only, but all Easterns measure life by a standard irreconcilable with that of the European, and when we put the influence of these two causes together we get a current of thought, native to the Moslem wherever he is found, no outside influence or power can stem or divert. And this being so, apart from all considerations of their respective political relations, it is evident that the Moslems and Christians of Egypt as of other countries could not be otherwise than opposed to each other, and that the very causes that made them so served to sever both alike from the French.

As Orientals the native Christians had, in spite of their differences, many thoughts and many habits and customs that they shared with the Moslems, but which were wholly unacceptable to the French. Nor were the French less disappointed by the attitude of the Moslems to them than were the Christians by that of the French towards them. They had expected from the French a preference they did not get, and a patronage that was withheld, while the openly professed friendship of Bonaparte for the Moslems and their religion was to them the act of a traitor and a renegade, and none the less so that they, like the Moslems, were by no means misled as to the real nature of the friendship or of its object.

Great as was the hatred of the Christians for the Moslems it was not, as we have seen, sufficient to prevent their joining these in their protest against a French reform that touched their own prejudices; but though that incident might have taught them that it would be to their own interests to conciliate Moslem feeling, so far from attempting anything of the kind they hastened to avail themselves of the collapse of the revolt to indulge in language and acts offensive to the Mahomedans.

Believing that the permanency of French rule was now assured, they abandoned all the restraints they had been compelled to submit to in the time of the *beys*, and which they had been more or less chary of neglecting under the early pro-Moslem policy of their successors. Having suffered but little from the event that had proved so disastrous to the Moslems, they had ample funds to enable them to follow their own inclinations, and, throwing aside the simple costumes and habits prescribed for them by the old law, went abroad clad in gold-embroidered garments, carrying weapons and mounted upon horses—all luxuries that had long been forbidden to them—and did not fail to flaunt their new-born liberty in the eyes of the Moslems, and openly exult in the discomfiture that had overtaken these.

Meanwhile a party of the French army was in constant pursuit of the fugitive Mamaluks, and small parties were being sent from Cairo to punish raiding Bedouins or villages that obstinately refused to pay the taxes imposed upon them. These latter always returned to Cairo with such booty of flocks and herds and other property as they had been able to obtain, all of which was appropriated to the use of the French. However excusable or even necessary this continuation of military operations may have been, it had a most disastrous effect upon the trade and commerce of the country. The small foreign trade that the country still possessed at the time of the invasion had ceased altogether, and the disturbed condition of the country had been almost equally fatal to local trade.

Communications between Cairo and distant towns, even Alexandria and Damietta, were rare and uncertain, and the attempts of the French to maintain a postal service between the scattered portions of the army had almost completely failed. As a consequence of the general disorder thus prevailing, the merchants and dealers of Cairo suffered so heavily that large numbers of them were reduced to indigency and compelled to seek a livelihood by any means that offered. Some who had contrived to save a small amount from the wreck of their business opened restaurants or coffee-houses, or took to the sale of fruits and cakes and other small articles that were in demand among the French, while yet others gained a living by hiring the donkeys they had once themselves ridden in state to the soldiers, who had taken to donkey-riding and racing as one of their chief amusements.

The approach of the second year of the occupation brought no change in the condition of affairs, but rumours of the coming of a Turkish army were growing not only more frequent but more consistent, and Bonaparte, believing that it would be better for him to assume the offensive than to await an attack, began to hasten the carrying out of preparations for the conquest of Syria. The prospect of active service was hailed with pleasure by the troops, but the native Christians were dismayed at the idea of any large body of the French army leaving the immediate vicinity of the town, fearing that the Moslems would seize the opportunity to avenge themselves for the insults and injuries they had been bearing at their hands.

Urged by this fear and with the idea of inducing Bonaparte to postpone his departure if not to abandon it altogether, some Syrians went to him and told him that the Moslems were preparing a new revolt. Fortunately for the Moslems these mischief-makers, in the excess of their cunning and anxiety to influence the French, gave a number of alleged details which Bonaparte at once saw afforded him a possibility of testing the truth of the information given. Some precautions were taken, but it was soon evident that the Moslems had no intention whatever of modifying in any way the pacific attitude they had assumed. Enraged at the attempt to mislead him, Bonaparte not only had the offenders arrested but issued an order that all the Syrians in the town were to resume the distinctive costume and be subjected to the other restrictions that had formerly been imposed upon them by the *beys*. The annual fast of the month of *Ramadan*, during which the Moslems abstain from eating, drinking, and smoking from early dawn until sunset, beginning about this time, a proclamation was issued forbidding all non-Moslems to eat, drink, or smoke in the streets, or in sight of those who were fasting, and a Christian who was caught smoking was promptly arrested and *bastinadoed*.

These and other concessions that were made to Moslem sentiment were not altogether unappreciated by them, but coming as they did at a time when, as they were well aware, the French had more than usual interest in gaining their goodwill, they could not but regard these things as the husks of the corn that the French were to eat, and saw, therefore, but little reason to be grateful for them, but they at least returned them in kind by according the French the passive submission they were so anxious for, and so, satisfied by the conduct of the people that he could safely withdraw the bulk of his army, Bonaparte started for Syria.

With the story of this ill-fated expedition we have nothing to do, for though usually given at great length in the histories of the country it forms no part of its history, the Egyptians having no further interest in it than that arising from their sympathy with the people attacked. They heard with pleasure of the difficulties and privations the army had to encounter and endure, with regret of its successes, and with sincere rejoicing of its ultimate discomfiture. It was in vain that Bonaparte sent them the most rose-coloured reports; no one accepted or believed them. The cold-blooded butchery of six thousand disarmed prisoners at Jaffa was an incident of the expedition which historians in vain try to gloss over or excuse, but with all the fawning fallacies with which they seek to save the honour of their hero, the massacre was one of the most brutal and inexcusable atrocities of all those that sully the pages of history.

No sophisms can defend it, for not only was there not the slightest ground for a plea of justification, but the measure was a stupid and impolitic blunder. The soldiers, we are told, carried out their revolting task of shooting down the bound and helpless victims with the greatest reluctance. It was a notable example of the power of discipline, the immediate, unquestioning obedience of the soldier; but such discipline as this! When we think of the men on the fast-sinking *Birkenhead* falling into rank and standing to order as the doomed vessel made her final plunge one feels that discipline may be great and glorious—but the discipline that stained the sands of Jaffa with the blood of six thousand unarmed, pinioned men!

Meanwhile the Ramadan having come to an end, the people of Cairo celebrated the *Eed*, or feast with which they return to the ordinary routine of life, in much the same way but with much less feasting and rejoicing than usual. According to the regular custom in all Mahomedan towns and villages, the people assembled on the first day of the feast to celebrate it with special prayers and thanksgivings, and we get a curious insight into their manner of regarding the ceremonies of their religion from an incident that occurred on this occasion. By some strange forgetfulness the Imam, or official leader of the prayers, omitted to recite the *Fatiha*, the prayer which is in Islam that which the *"Lord's Prayer"* is in the Christian Church, with the addition that it is always recited as the opening prayer whenever and wherever Moslems worship.

Under all ordinary circumstances the Moslem idea of propriety in a mosque or place of prayer is such as prevails in the churches of Europe, but the reverent attention that is customarily given to the Imam will not stand any great strain and so, reminded by a storm of protests from the thousands of worshippers present, the Imam on this occasion had to recommence the service! Let the reader try and imagine the congregation at some great festival in St. Paul's or St. Peter's roaring at his Grace the Archbishop of Canterbury, or his Holiness the Pope that he had omitted the collect for the day, and peremptorily ordering him to recommence the service!

Two months later, in May, 1799, the great *Eed*, or day of sacrifice, was kept, but in this as in all things the shadow of the French occupation overhung the people and embittered their feelings. Sheep, which for several reasons are the animals generally chosen for sacrifice, could not be had, partly because the flocks of the neighbouring villages had been almost wholly consumed by the French and partly because the restless condition of the country prevented those of more distant places being sent into the town. So the salvos of artillery with which according to custom the occasion was celebrated were listened to by the people but failed to awaken the usual enthusiasm, and, fired as they were by the unorthodox hands of the French gunners, were to the

Moslems little better than a mockery.

Early in the year when the plague had first appeared rigorous police regulations had been issued for the protection of the French, who suffered from the dread of epidemics so universal in Christian Europe, but which, as readers of Kinglake's *Eothen* will remember, so slightly disturb the Oriental mind.

As the year had advanced the plague had shown no signs of disappearing, and new and more stringent orders were issued in the hope of restricting it. Dire penalties were therefore imposed for concealing a case or a death, or for neglecting the prescribed sanitary precautions, and some idea of the frantic terror that possessed the compilers of these regulations may be gathered from the fact that death was the punishment proclaimed for any one sick of the plague who should dare enter any other house than his own dwelling.

Thus the first year of the French occupation and the year of the Moslem calendar came to an end within a few days of each other, and Gabarty winds up his long and yet all too brief record of the woes and tribulations of the twelve months by saying that it had been full of "unheard-of events, the most important being that the people of Egypt had been unable to make the pilgrimage to Mecca!"

A very notable conclusion of the year's story—a conclusion that tells us much of the people and their most extraordinary and irrational way, as you no doubt think it, of looking upon the affairs of life. The coming of the French, the terrible sufferings of the panic-stricken town, the gathering of that wild storm of revolt, its bursting, collapse, the long-delayed hope of relief, the daily outraging of the most cherished prejudices of the people—all these, the great flood of evil and sorrow that was the one recollection of that miserable time for all the people—all this was of less importance than the fact that a few hundred individuals had been unable to perform the dangerous journey to Mecca!

Death, want, misfortune and misery of every kind had filled the record of the year for one and all of the people, but this one thing in which but a few of them only could have any direct personal interest, this was "the most important event of the year!"

Is it any wonder that the people refused to fall down and worship the golden calf of the French Republic that Bonaparte and his Staff were so vainly trying to exalt!

That the reader may the more justly appreciate Gabarty's comment on the history of the year he must recall two facts with reference to the composition of his history—first that it was written at the time. It is not a record compiled in after years when the feelings, emotions, and thoughts of the moment had been forgotten or blurred, It was rather a diary scribbled down from day to day, and one written, too, with no special object other than that of recording the principal occurrences of the time.

A mere narrative, not written in support of a theory, nor as a study of men or things, nor as a text for the exposition of the author's views, but simply in the plainest and most literal sense a mere narrative. Secondly, it is not as an opinion but as a fact that he puts this failure of the pilgrimage down as the most important event of that disastrous year. And he puts it down as a fact in terms that show clearly that he believes that as a matter of opinion it is one no one who may ever read his history will for a moment think of questioning or doubting in any way.

If the reader can by any possibility bring himself to comprehend in the faintest degree the true purport of this summing up of the year's history he will have got a long, a very long, way on the road to a clear comprehension of the Egyptian as he was in 1798, and as he still is.

It may help the reader somewhat to form some idea of his own on this subject if I turn aside for a moment to tell him what this pilgrimage to Mecca is, and how it is regarded by the Moslems of Egypt and other countries.

Itself surrounded by the hills of the desert district of the Hegaz, the city of Mecca has grown around and encircles a great rectangular open but cloister-bounded space, in the centre of which rises a flat-roofed building occupying a mere spot in the vast courtyard, and which, but for its height, might be termed a cube, clothed on all sides by a hanging cloth of the deepest black, relieved only by a band of Arabic lettering wrought in gold. Nature herself has produced no more impressive sight than that presented by this small building thus strangely garbed and hid away in the wastes of the desert. In size, in form, in all things save its sable garment gently swaying to the slightest breeze, the building is one that would never draw from the stranger a second glance, but as it is, once seen it dwells upon the mind for ever with a vividness of detail no other sight can produce.

This is the *Beit Allah*, the "House of God" of Islam, first erected, as Moslem tradition relates, by the Prophet Abrahim, and ever since a place of pilgrimage for all true worshippers of God. Hither while yet Christianity and Islam were yet unknown, in the "days of ignorance," when the Arabs still worshipped idols of stone, they came from all parts of the Arab-speaking world as pilgrims, counting all the many dangers of the road as nought compared to the rich rewards awaiting in the future those who should accomplish this duty.

Enjoined upon the Moslems as one of the five great obligations of their creed, the pilgrimage today draws Moslems from the most distant parts of the world by long and tedious journeys through the wildest and least-civilised parts of the earth, heedless of dangers and difficulties, counting it a gain to suffer by the way, and content to die once their eyes have fallen upon the sacred building. And of all Moslems the Egyptian, and most especially the Cairene, has a special and peculiar interest in the pilgrimage since it is the privilege of Cairo to supply from year to year the new *kiswa*, or clothing for the *Beit Allah*.

Here, then, we have a partial clue to the importance attached to the failure of the pilgrimage by the Cairenes, but, as I have said, the failure was one that directly affected but a few hundreds of the people— those who under more favourable circumstances would have taken part in the pilgrimage. But these, from the point of view of their own pilgrimage, would accept the impossibility of performing it in that year as a matter of destiny, and would have regarded the impoverishment of their resources caused by the endless exactions of the French as a greater evil, as one not only preventing their making the pilgrimage in that year, but possibly also in future years, since the expenses of the journey are such that to the ordinary pilgrim they are only to be met by the economy of years.

There was, therefore, some other reason why the failure of the pilgrimage should be looked upon as so great a calamity, and if the reader will recall the incident of the omitted prayer at the festival of the *Eed*, it may assist in guiding him to the solution of the problem, for in that incident we get an aid to the understanding of the Egyptian's attitude towards his religion and his interpretation of its duties. This and other matters that I have had occasion to speak of may perhaps enable the reader to understand at least this much—that this people has a standard of good and evil very different to his own, and that no scale of weal and woe that he could draw out would be at all likely to commend itself to their acceptance.

He who has grasped this fact will have gained a position from which he may hope to pursue his study of the Egyptians and their history, with at least one solid, indisputable fact to guide him—a fact that, almost impossible as one would think it to be, the ordinary historian of the country seems quite unable to realise. It is true that in so many set words or phrases they tell their readers that the Egyptian does not reason or think as other men do, but having said so much they describe and criticise their actions and thoughts without the least reference to this fundamental and controlling fact. Nor is it the historians alone who make this crass mistake. Men living in the country, nay, even those born and reared in it, and living in the closest intimacy with Egyptians, are no wiser, and hence, whenever Egyptian thought or opinion run counter to their own, they all agree in attributing the difference to "stupidity" or "fanaticism."

And what is still less realised is that this difference is not limited to the Moslems, but is shared by the Christians of the country. Severed from each other as the Moslem and Eastern Christian are in thought and aspiration, they are, though not wholly one, strongly sympathetic in their estimates of European civilisation as it is commonly presented to them. The active effect of their sympathy is partly nullified by the interest the Christian has in seeing the predominant power in the hands of his coreligionists, and it was this interest, and this interest alone, and not any sympathy with French views or French ideals, that gained from the Christians of Egypt whatever of support they gave the French. In all books on the East it is tacitly assumed by the writers that were the East Christianised it would be in full sympathy with European thought.

No greater error is conceivable. The Coptic or the Syrian clerk in the service of the Egyptian Government of today, compelled as he is by the official regulations, attends his office in European dress, but goes home to throw that off at the first possible moment to resume the garb of the country, the loose, flowing garments that good sense and experience alike tell him are not only the most comfortable but the most healthy in a climate such as that of Egypt. And as in this so in other things. Like the Moslem, he accepts many of the comforts and conventions of European life, but like him he rejects not a few of these that north of the Mediterranean are deemed indispensable.

These were things that the French did not and perhaps could not see. And there was yet another obstacle they had to surmount, but of the presence of which they seem to have been oblivious. The civilisation that the French wished to plant in Egypt had not been the growth of a day, but the fruit of centuries of slow and halting progress. Had it been possible for a foreign power to have attempted to introduce that civilisation into France, say in the ninth or tenth century, what manner of reception would it have had? Think you that the French people of that time would have hailed the innovations forced upon them with rapturous delight? that they would at once have appreciated every little detail, and hastened to abandon all their time-honoured habits and customs to adopt those of their new teachers?

How did our Hereward the Wake look upon the innovations of the Norman Conqueror? Was it with an ecstasy of admiration that Gurth the swineherd thought of the Norman civilisation of his day? Was it enthusiasm for the benefits advancing civilisation was bestowing upon them that led the Luddites in their machine-wrecking riots? The parallels are not perfect I admit, yet there is in them a sufficient resemblance of circumstance and fact to justify the comparison, and more than enough to discredit the conclusions that so many authors have drawn from the attitude of the people of Egypt towards the French.

We have not reached the pleasant lands of our modern civilisation wafted by a gentle breeze on a smoothly gliding bark, but have won our way through storm and tempest by paths bedewed with blood and tears, and withal our progress has been less a striving for good than a flight from evil, and though we are not perhaps all sensible of it, our appreciation of our civilisation is largely our appreciation of our triumph over evils and difficulties. The ignorant and thoughtless, whether of the "Smart Set" or of the slums, do not see this. They and all of their class take life, as do their cats and dogs and the beasts of the field, as they find it. Yet he who can and will think must admit that it is so, and, admitting this, will see that in addition to the other causes that prevented the Egyptians accepting the French and their reforms there was this very important one, that they could not in any way appreciate them as reforms, seeing that they were not yet conscious of the existence of the evils they were intended to remedy.

To the Egyptian, as I have said before, the life he had been living under the Mamaluks needed but little to make it perfect. Moderate taxation and the abolition of the erratic tyranny from which the people suffered were the two things wanted to make his life wholly desirable and pleasant. These evils, so far from being abolished by the French, were, in the opinion of the Egyptian, increased a hundredfold. And to these the French added a host of minor evils: worrying and wearisome regulations, cramping the liberty and freedom the people had always enjoyed, thwarting their natural instincts and burthening them with a sense of control they had never before experienced.

Again, I ask, what wonder was it that they did not fall down and worship the golden calf of the Republic?

CHAPTER 13

The Siege of Cairo

It was the middle of June, 1799, before Bonaparte got back to Cairo from Syria. His prolonged siege of Acre had been an utter failure, and save for a little worthless loot the whole expedition had been but a sample of that which his whole life was to be—a selfish, reckless waste of human life, useless, unprofitable, and, in spite of the servile adulation it has had, entirely contemptible. That this man was personally brave, skilful in war, a clever general—in short, that he was a man of many abilities that, rightly exercised, would have entitled him to respect and admiration—is perfectly true, but it is not more true of him than of many that the world has rightly and properly agreed to class as criminals. Seeking nothing but his own gain, in this futile expedition he had sacrificed thousands of lives, wrecked hundreds of innocent homes. More than a third of his army had perished, including twelve hundred of his sick and wounded abandoned to the vengeance of the enemy for his own ruthless slaughter of his prisoners. Such is the great hero of modern civilisation!

But defeated and discomfited as he was, he entered Cairo in triumph with banners flying, drums beating, and all the rest of the idle fanfaronade and pompous puerilities associated with triumphal entries. Five long hours the grand procession occupied in passing through the city gates, and thenceforth for three days and nights his coming was celebrated with loud rejoicings and feastings, and the Egyptians looked on and even took such part in the hollow mockery as they were commanded to do, but they were in no way deceived; the gaunt skeleton of defeat and failure was clothed but not concealed by the gaudy glare of lying pretence.

So the "Great" Bonaparte paid honour to himself, heedless of the droning of the surges on St. Helena's distant shore.

A month later the long-expected Turkish army arrived by sea, and, landing at Abou Kir on the 14th of July, was besieged by the French under Bonaparte himself on the 25th. Although aided by Sir Sidney Smith, who was in command of a fleet that had already assisted in the defence of Acre, the Turks, defeated by starvation, had to yield on the 2nd of August.

The news of the arrival of the Turks had been received in Cairo with unbounded joy, though none but a few of the hot-headed lower classes had given any open expression to their feelings, but when Bonaparte returned to the city with a long file of Turkish prisoners the despondency of the people was overwhelming; yet, though it was felt by all to be a rebinding of the chains of their bondage, they gave no sign, and the life of the town went on in the listless way that was becoming habitual to it. It was the easier for the people to bear this reverse that they by no means looked upon it as in any way a final one. The defeat of the Turks was but the defeat of a small force taken at great disadvantage, and one which they did not doubt was but the advance guard of an army against which the French could make no stand.

Meanwhile, the period of the inundation having arrived, the rising of the Nile was celebrated by order, as it had been the year before, but this time with an abandon on the part of the Christians that gravely shocked Gabarty, who tells us that the eve of the *fête* was spent by them in boats on the river, or in the open along its banks, with feasting and drinking and women and music.

> On this occasion they forgot their self-respect and cast modesty aside for indecency, raillery, impudence, and impiety. The pen refuses to paint the scandals of the night. Licence was carried to its extreme, and the dregs of the people, following the example set them, the debauchery and effrontery were without limit.

All night the Bacchanalian festival was continued, the outrageous orgy ceasing only with the utter exhaustion of the degraded devotees of pleasure.

Some four days later Bonaparte gave a fresh proof of his greatness by deserting the army that had served him so faithfully, and, abandoning his dream of founding an Eastern Empire, hastened back to Europe to pursue with unabated enthusiasm his own selfish ambitions. His departure, like his coming and all his stay, was accompanied by the silly rigmarole of braggart falsehoods he was never tired of issuing, and which deceived no one but himself. He was going, so he said, to open communications with France, and was to return in three months to exterminate "the enemies of order."

Under General Kleber, whom Bonaparte had named as his successor in the command of the French army, matters went smoothly enough, although he was less affable in his treatment of the natives than Bonaparte had been. He, like all the French, was heartily sick of the country, and longing for an opportunity of escaping from it. The first glamour of the occupation had long since passed away, and the dreary monotony of their lives, coupled with the debilitating effect of the climate, needed only the cowardly desertion of their chief to plunge the French into a state of deep despondency. The task entrusted to General Kleber was one, therefore, sufficient to try the ablest, and it was not lessened by the complete destruction of trade and commerce, the heavy expenses of the army, and the difficulty of dragging any further large supplies from the impoverished people.

It is not surprising, therefore, that when the arrival of a Turkish army from Syria was announced, the general hastened to accept the offer of the English admiral to give the French army a safe and honourable opportunity of retiring. A convention was signed by which it was agreed that the French were to evacuate the country within three months. This being promptly made known to the Egyptians, the people rejoiced openly and without restraint, the lower classes going so far as to insult and abuse the French to their faces, to the great indignation of Gabarty, who does not fail to condemn their conduct not only as foolish but as unworthy of a self-respecting people. A few days later a Turkish officer arrived, and was received with rapturous acclamations.

The day following the Vizier Yosuf, who was in command of the Turkish forces, issued his first orders to the people through the mouth of the officer they had thus cordially welcomed. Nothing could well be briefer or more explicit than these orders. They were but two in number, and were, first, that the people were to receive the officer in question as Chief of Customs, with the power of establishing monopolies of all food supplies; and secondly, the immediate raising of a sum of three thousand purses, to be paid to the French as a contribution towards the expenses of their evacuation of the country. "Thus," says the always candid Gabarty, "from the first moment the country had to suffer two evils at the hands of the Turks." But the tax levied was quickly collected, the people paying gladly to hasten the departure of the French. "Blessed be the day on which the *infidel* dogs quit us," was the cry raised, loudest of all by those who had most availed themselves of the presence of the French to indulge in a laxity of living offensive to all the better classes.

Notwithstanding the reminder the people had so promptly received that the Turks, however much they were to be preferred to the French, were by no means lenient rulers, the rejoicings for their coming were universal among the Moslems, and though there were not a few of the more enlightened and sensible who were wise and bold enough to protest against the offensive treatment of the French, the current of popular feeling was too strong, and carried with it even men who had heretofore kept their heads. So once more the children of the schools were led by their masters through the streets, as they had been at the first arrival of the French, chanting songs in derision of, or of malediction on, the hated *feringhees*.

But if the Moslems were exultant, the Christians of the town were plunged in despondency and were keenly lamenting the folly that had led them to outrage Moslem sentiment in the manner they had done. Fearful that in the excited state of the people these would now seek to avenge the wanton insults that had been offered them, they withdrew from the streets and public places and hid in their houses, awaited in trembling fear the attack they anticipated would be made upon them. But the people were thinking of other things, and were too full of joy at the promise of their early escape from the bitter thraldom of the French to have a thought to spare for the minor grievances which they had endured from their Christian countrymen, and so these were left in peace.

Meanwhile small parties of the Turkish troops began to enter the town, and these, according to a pleasant custom that survives in the Turkish army up to the present day in outlying parts of the Empire, at once proceeded to constitute themselves partners in the commercial affairs of the people, without the aid of notaries or anything more than the very simplest of procedures. Seating themselves on the *mustabahs*, or raised fronts of the shops that serve at once as seats for the customers and counters for the display of the shopman's goods, they simply waited until a customer arrived and then demanded from the shopkeeper a share of his profits, alleging, not always untruthfully, that they had assisted in the sale of the goods by praising their quality, cheapness, and so forth, and, when a customer appeared unconvinced, not unfrequently by threatening him with violence should he refuse to complete a purchase.

Needless to say, customers and dealers alike soon learned to shun the transaction of business in the presence of these "partners." Complaints were made to the new governor of the town, but the only satisfaction accorded to the indignant plaintiffs was that they ought to be pleased at the opportunity of contributing to the upkeep of the troops that had come to defend them from the French and free the country from their *infidel* rule.

Eager as the people were to be rid of the French, these were not less so to get away from a town that no longer had any charm for them, and was associated with so much of disappointment. The work, therefore, of preparing for the evacuation was carried on with goodwill, and the citadel and the forts around the town were handed over to the Turks, while the French assembled themselves in camps in and about the Esbekieh.

The three months allowed for the evacuation was drawing to a close when the folly of the British Government suddenly altered the whole position. The convention which Sir Sidney Smith had accorded the French had been drawn up on a thorough understanding of the actual facts with which he had to deal. Knowing well that it was entirely out of his power to dictate terms to the French, and realising how greatly it would be to the advantage of his own country that the French should retire, he had treated with Kleber rather as a friend than as an enemy. But the government, with absolutely nothing to guide it but Sir Sidney's report, declined to listen to his advice or to accept the action he had taken, and ordered him to insist upon the French making an unconditional surrender.

A wiser and stronger man than Sir Sidney would have ignored instructions so fatal to the honour and interests of his own country, and so gratuitously insulting to brave and honourable foes; but, to the great misfortune of all concerned, Sir Sidney had not the courage to do justice to himself, and so communicated the decision of the government to General Kleber. The blow was a bitter one. Honourable as the convention he had accepted had been, it had demanded some sacrifice of pride on the part of the French to adopt it, and Kleber was perfectly justified in terming the demand now made "insolent."

Thus the madness of our government at the moment when the French were straining every nerve to leave the country, forced them to remain, and not only gave them fresh and good reason to detest us, but laid a train of anti-English feeling in Egypt that bears consequences prejudicial to English interests even to the present day.

Finding his hope of an early return to Europe thus shattered, Kleber took the only line of action open to him, and showed his ability as a general by immediately re-entering the forts around the city which the Turks, finding a residence in the town itself more in accordance with their ideas of comfort, had neglected to occupy. This done, he hastened to attack the Turkish Army, which was encamped at Materiah, some five miles from the town, and taking it by surprise and wholly unprepared for action, believing itself in peaceful and unthreatened possession of the country, routed it with ease and without loss.

This attack was naturally regarded as a most treacherous one by the Turks and Egyptians, for until the French had actually opened fire upon the Turks these had remained in careless security without the least suspicion that anything could occur to bring them into conflict with the French. But it is quite impossible to blame Kleber. For the French an early and complete victory was now a matter of life and death. To have given the Turks an opportunity of attacking them in the forts around Cairo would have been suicidal madness. With no possibility of relief they could only have held out against a siege until the sickness and famine that were bound to assail them should have accomplished the work of the enemy more effectually than its military strength could.

As the time fixed for the evacuation had approached the excitement in the town had increased, but when the French re-seized the forts and gave other proofs of a sudden activity in a new and, to the Egyptians, wholly inexplicable direction, rumours of the wildest kind were circulated. Of these the one that gained most credence was that the French had discovered it to be the intention of the Turks and the English to surround and massacre them while on their way to the coast. Utterly false as this report was, the outbreak of hostilities between the French and the Turks gave it such apparent verification, that there are not a few of the Egyptians who still believe it.

The Turkish Army, utterly discomfited by the French, after having made but a poor defence, took the road towards Syria, with the exception of a part which, finding itself between the French and the town, decided to seek the shelter of the latter. With these were a number of Mamaluk *beys* and their followers, who at the first news of the arrival of the Turks had hastened to join them. The Turks who thus entered the town were under the command of Nasooh Pacha, a bigot and fanatic of high rank but little ability. His arrival was greeted by the assembling of a crowd of all the worst characters of the town, who flocked after him as he made his way through the streets, anxious to learn the truth as to what had happened. His first act was to give a general but definite order for the massacre of all the Christians.

We have seen how at the last meeting of the Mamaluk Dewan, and again at Rosetta, proposals to massacre the Christians had been rejected. Now, however, there was no question of a proposal, but a distinct and definite order was given by a *pacha*, a Turk, an orthodox Moslem, a high officer of the empire, and one who at the moment carried with him all the weight of being the immediate representative of the *sultan* and *caliph* of Islam. Those of the people to whom the order was given were of the lowest and most ignorant class, precisely the one to which such an order might be expected to be welcome, people having nothing to risk but their personal safety, and thinking little of this as weighed against the prospect of a rich harvest of loot.

A wild rush was made, therefore, for the Christian quarters of the town, the mob slaying on its way the few Christians who happened to be overtaken by it and unable to escape. Hastily barricading their doors and windows the Christians made a bold stand, and the mob, which was much more anxious to plunder the houses than to slaughter their inhabitants, devoted their unwelcome attentions to the least protected of these, and troubling nothing as to whether the houses attacked were those of Christians or Moslems, were busily engaged in their work of destruction when the quarters in which they were, were swept by Turkish troops, who, without staying to expostulate or explain, quickly routed the rioters with much heavier slaughter than these had been guilty of, and charging them, more ruthlessly and more effectively than they had charged the Christians, promptly restored order.

This vigorous suppression of the riot and intended massacre was the work of Osman Agha, an officer of the Turkish army who, though of less degree than Nasooh Pacha, had no sooner heard of the riot than he protested not merely by word of mouth, but by the more practical measure of despatching troops in hot haste with strict orders to spare none of the rioters that did not at once desist. Thus once more the Christians found Moslem protectors ready to defend them against Moslem foes. We shall see later on how the Christians showed their gratitude.

The riot having been thus promptly suppressed, the Turkish officers turned their attention to the defence of the town from the attack by the French, which they rightly judged would not long be delayed. A hurried survey of the available means of defence showed that these were of the poorest. Gunpowder and munitions of all kinds were deficient in quantity and defective in quality, but there was no thought of submission to the coming foe, and, directed by the troops, the people were set to work once more to barricade the entrances to the town. The memories of the sufferings that had accompanied and followed the great revolt against the French were still vivid in the minds of the people, but their enthusiasm was as great as it had been while yet the horrors of a siege were unknown to and undreamt of by them. Some of the Mamaluk chiefs, seeing how woefully the town was deficient in the things most urgently needed to enable it to make a stand, were anxious to withdraw, but neither the Turkish troops nor the people would consent to their doing so, and they had perforce to remain and take their part in the defence.

Fighting was commenced by an attack upon the house of Elfi Bey, in the Esbekieh quarter, which Bonaparte having chosen as his residence was still in the occupation of the French. One day's firing having exhausted the supply of cannon-ball, the defect was made good for the moment by charging the guns with metal weights collected from the shops in the bazaars, and such other missiles as could be found. Under the direction of Osman Agha, shot and powder factories were established, and all the craftsmen of the town whose skill could be applied to the manufacture of defensive arms or materials were put to work to provide what was needed, or the best substitute that could be improvised. Being unable to ascertain anything of the movements or intentions of the French, the chiefs decided that it was imperatively necessary to be ready for an assault upon the town at any moment. Orders were given, therefore, that all the townsmen as well as the troops were to take up positions behind or near the barricades, and were to remain on the spot day and night, sleeping as best they could at their posts.

For eight days the fighting was continued in this way, the firing being confined to the north-west end of the town, or that facing the position occupied by the French. On the eighth day the return of General Kleber, who had been in pursuit of the flying Turkish Army, brought about a change. With the troops he had with him, and those already in garrison, he had a force quite equal to the siege of the town in regular form, and he lost no time in surrounding the two towns, Cairo and Boulac, as Gabarty expresses it, "as a bracelet encircles the arms." Thenceforth the siege was carried on with vigour. Amply provided with arms and ammunition, the French poured a ceaseless hail of shot and shell upon the towns, not only from the forts around, but also from the heights of the Mokattam hills, which command the greater part of the city of Cairo.

For ten days and nights the siege and bombardment went on unceasingly. For ten days and nights the people and the troops were without any rest worthy of the name, and the long strain was beginning to tell upon their energies. To add to the horrors of the bombardment under which the buildings of the town were steadily crumbling away and filling the streets with their ruins, not only was death busy, but hunger and thirst were beginning to assail the living. Food was not only scarce, but what there was was ruthlessly appropriated by the Turkish troops, and the water was not only short but bad.

Still, all ranks kept manfully to their task, and while the lower classes laboured cheerfully at what work there was for them to do, in clearing the streets of the wreckage that threatened to block them entirely, and in attending upon the troops, carrying ammunition to and fro as needed, and so on, the highest of the Turks and Egyptians moved constantly among them, encouraging them and bidding them hope for the best. Of the Christians many had escaped from the town to seek shelter with the French, in whose ultimate triumph they had the fullest and withal most justifiable confidence. Of those that remained in the town, not a few lent what aid they could to its defence, partly to conciliate the mob and partly no doubt in recognition of the protection given them by the leaders of the people, as evidence of their loyalty to the *sultan*, and as the line of conduct most likely to conduce to their own interests.

Many who under the Mamaluks had grown wealthy and under the French had escaped having to bear anything like their fair share of the burthens laid upon the people, now bid for popularity by contributing funds towards the defence. But the steadily growing weakness of their position, the exhaustion of the people and the troops, and the prospect of an utter failure of food and other supplies compelled the leaders to think of making terms with the French while they were yet in a position to profit from whatever concessions they could obtain. And the French knowing pretty well how things were going in the city, and having no desire for useless bloodshed, made repeated offers to treat. But the people would hear nothing of a surrender, and nothing of treating for terms. They had had enough of the French, and would have no more of them, if by any means, by any sacrifice, they could get rid of them.

The Turkish *vizier* with his army was sure to come to their relief soon, and perhaps the English, for were not the English the enemies of the French? And Mourad Bey with a large force of Mamaluks and troops was not far off, and he too must come sooner or later to their aid. So they would rather starve and thirst and suffer until help came; and besides, was it not evident that the French must be nearly exhausted? if not, why did they offer terms?

At last the chiefs took action for themselves, and a deputation of *sheikhs* was sent out to the French headquarters to treat for terms.

Kleber received the deputation courteously, but reproached them for having taken the part of the Turks, and given these their aid and support. The *sheikhs* very justly replied that they had but followed the advice he had himself given them when announcing the approaching departure of the French. Eventually it was agreed that there should be a truce of three days to enable the Turkish troops and all who cared to go with them to leave the town. "As to the people," said Kleber, "they have nothing to fear; are they not our people?"

Full of hope and joy at the result of their mission, the *sheikhs* returned to report what they believed would be accepted as good news by the famine-stricken garrison. But far from accepting the terms offered, the people insulted the *sheikhs* and denounced them as traitors. "If," said they, "the Christian dogs were not at the end of their resources they would not be so ready to make peace." So fighting was resumed, and carried on on both sides with vigour until the 25th of April.

Boulac was the first to fall. A heavy thunderstorm had broken over the devoted towns, and torrents of rain had quickly converted their unpaved streets into quagmires, that rendered walking almost impossible. With abundance of skill and material at their disposal, and in robust health and spirits, the French had every advantage over the famished, exhausted and undisciplined mob that had so long faced them at such desperate odds, yet it was but foot by foot only that they succeeded in forcing their way to victory through streets heaped with the bodies of the slain.

It was a heroic fight, that of this poor famine-pinched, undisciplined mob against the well-fed, well-clothed veterans of France. Strange that our friends the historians, who are always so impartial and free from bigotry and fanaticism, can see in this desperate defence nothing more than the contumacy of an ignorant and foolish people. Strange, for, after all, "how can man die better than facing fearful odds, for the ashes of his fathers, and the temples of their gods?" For this in the very literal sense of the words was what these poor starving Egyptians were doing, it being not the least of their complaints against the French that these had desecrated the graveyards of the city, and defiled the temple in which they worshipped God.

A wild carnival of pillage and brutality followed the fall of the town, and then the troops that had been investing Boulac turned with revived appetite to assist in the siege of Cairo. There, as at Boulac, the scarcity of food and water, and the want of proper rest and shelter, had reduced the people to a condition that would have justified their abandoning the hopeless struggle without further effort; yet it was not the people, but their chiefs—the Mamaluk *beys* and the Turkish officers—men whose experience told them how unavailing the attempt to hold out must prove, that spoke or thought of treating with the foe. They had, as we have seen, already made an effort in that direction, now, finding the French gradually gaining ground, pushing their way slowly but surely into the town and, to add fresh terrors to those by which the unhappy defenders were almost overwhelmed, firing the houses as fast as they could reach them, the chiefs once more asked for terms, and were accorded three days in which to quit the town.

Even then the people would have refused to yield, and it was with difficulty that their leaders at last forced from them a sullen and unwilling submission. Kleber, in addition to granting the Turks and Mamaluks three days within which to evacuate the town, undertook to supply funds and transport to enable them to go, but demanded the exchange of hostages. All who wished were to be free to depart with the retiring troops. These were liberal terms, but still the people were unwilling to submit, and when the French hostages arrived they had to be protected by a large body of the Turkish troops, and even Osman Agha himself, who throughout the siege had been foremost in the defence, and ever where danger was thickest, even he had to seek protection from the wrath of the mob that still furiously cried out against the admission of the French.

At length, peace and order having been restored, the Turks and Mamaluks made haste to leave the town, and a general amnesty having been proclaimed, Cairo was once more treated to a grand triumphal entry of the French, and was once more directed to decorate and illuminate itself in token of rejoicing.

For the third time the people settled down to bear the rule of the French with what patience they could, and, in the manner that still characterises their daily lives, the quarrel of the moment having been abandoned, they let it sleep and went about their affairs as much as possible as if nothing had ever occurred to interrupt them. Not that they were in the least reconciled to the French, or that they had ceased to long for redemption from the slavery in which they were held. Far from that, but loyal to the terms they had accepted, they desisted from all open or, indeed, covert opposition. It would have been unreasonable to ask or expect more than this. So the truce having once been made the French, though they did not think so, were absolutely safe from any molestation or annoyance from the people who, as a body, with all their faults, fear God, and, obeying the law of Islam, observe their covenants even when made with an enemy.

One might have thought that this people, who had so strenuously resisted the making of peace, who had turned against the most trusted of their own leaders for accepting terms, who, in the hope of rendering peace impossible, had frantically attempted to attack the hostages—one might have thought that this people would have repudiated the terms, and have sought every opportunity to injure and annoy the French. Nor could they with any reason have been held altogether blameable in refusing to abide by terms made in direct opposition to their wishes. Yet this is, as I have said, just what they did not do, and peace once established, the French went about among them as safe and as free from molestation as though the people had no grievance against them.

Let us turn now and see how the French interpreted the amnesty they had accorded the people.

CHAPTER 14

The Price of Peace

"They have nothing to fear; are they not our people?"

Was it possible for the people of Cairo to have any better assurance than these words of General Kleber, that the "*Aman*," or amnesty, that was so loudly proclaimed and, by the French, so enthusiastically celebrated, was to be the full and free "*Aman*" which alone is understood by Oriental peoples? One would have thought not, but the Cairenes were to learn differently. They were to be taught that "amnesty" is a word which, like so many others, may be interpreted in varying senses, and that it has no other meaning than that which the user chooses to accord to it.

Among the rejoicings for the great victory of a strong, well-supplied, and well-nourished army of well-trained and disciplined veterans over a famished, half-naked, wholly undisciplined, and almost wholly exhausted mob of civilians, there had been, among other things, a great banquet, to which all the notables of the town were invited, and at which they were received by Kleber in a gracious manner—so gracious, indeed, that they went away full of pleasant dreams for the future. General Kleber had taken the opportunity to invite a number of the *ulema* to meet him on the following Friday morning, and believing that it was his intention, as indeed he had declared it to be, to discuss with them the revival of the *dewan* and other matters, they did not fail to appear punctually at the appointed time, some of them looking forward to receiving some recognition of their services in the promotion of peace. Arrived at the general's, they were not long in learning that the gala costume with which they had honoured the occasion was most unhappily inappropriate.

As a first intimation of the vanity of their hopes they were kept waiting in an ante-chamber until their patience was almost exhausted.

At length Kleber entered, and without any words of welcome or apology straightway proceeded once more to censure them for having allied themselves with the Turks. When the *sheikhs* once more protested that they had done so under his own instructions, given at the time that he had announced the approaching departure of the French, he blamed them for not having suppressed the "insurrection." They replied that this was wholly out of their power, and that those who, as he was aware, had made an effort to stop the fighting had been rudely treated, and even roughly handled, by the people. But it was the old story of the wolf and the lamb. Kleber was determined to bring the *sheikhs* in guilty in any case, and upbraided them with being double-faced.

This was not what the poor *sheikhs*, who had honestly done their best in the cause of peace, had expected as the reward of their efforts, or as the natural sequence of the courtesies extended to them at the banquet. All this, however, was but the preface to the announcement of what was, in fact, the real object of their being summoned to meet the general. This was nothing less than the seizing the *sheikhs* as hostages for the payment by the city of an enormous indemnity and the infliction of exorbitant fines upon each of five of the leading *sheikhs*. While yet the *sheikhs*, dumbfoundered by this novel interpretation of the word "amnesty," were trying to assure themselves that they were not the victims of an ill-timed jest, the general left the room as abruptly as he had entered it, and the *sheikhs* found that they were prisoners.

When at length, late in the evening, the sorely-troubled *sheikhs* had recovered somewhat from the consternation into which they had been thrown by the general's treatment of them, and the extravagance of the demand he had made, they proceeded to draw up classified lists of the inhabitants of the town and fix the sums that each class was to contribute towards the payment of the indemnity. As a basis upon which to allot the debt householders were assessed at a year's rent, and every trade, business, and industry in the town, down to the street musicians, jesters, and jugglers, was called upon to pay its share. This done the *sheikhs* were, with the exception of a few who were to be imprisoned until they had paid the special fines inflicted upon them, released, but under military guard. Among those imprisoned was the Sheikh el Sadat, the chief of the *Shereefs*, or descendants of the Prophet, upon whom a fine of 500,000 dollars had been imposed.

Then began the darkest days in the history of the country. Thenceforth tyranny and torture of every kind was adopted to force the payment of the indemnity, and all that the superior civilisation of France had to offer the wretched people to whom they had accorded an "amnesty," and whom they termed "our people," was the introduction of refinements in the tortures inflicted upon them, such as the bringing of the wife of the Sheikh el Sadat to witness the tortures inflicted upon her husband.

Historians glide lightly over this part of their story, and being perforce compelled to mention some of these incidents, are not ashamed to stoop to the contemptible excuse that such things were "the custom of the East," that the French were only availing themselves of the means that would have been employed against themselves in like case. Indeed, this was the excuse the French offered at the time. "Living in the East," said Vigo Roussillon, one of those present at the massacre of the Turkish prisoners at Jaffa, "we adopted the morals of the East."

There is an old chemical experiment in which the mixing of two coloured fluids produces a clear, transparent one, but no such experiment is possible in morality. Evil-doing is evil-doing, and neither the casuistry of the Jesuits nor the art of man can make it good or right doing. I myself believe that all evil eventually produces good—"*That every cloud that spreads above and veileth love, itself is love;*" but that affords no excuse for evil-doing. Nor could the French have found a falser or more barren excuse than this one. It is true that in the East, as in the West, tyranny and torture had been for ages the tools of tyrants, but those tyrants had in using those tools done so ignorantly and stupidly because they knew no better. They acted upon the natural impulse of men who knew no law but that of force, no right but that of the sword, no morality but their own pleasure, and as the circumstances and conditions of the times seemed to them to dictate.

They had no sense of doing evil. To them there was no other way of influencing men against their wills save by physical or mental pain, and they acted accordingly. It was quite otherwise with the French. They, with a perfect knowledge of what they were doing, did this evil, knowing it to be evil, and they did it deliberately, not in a moment of anger but with cool, thoughtful determination, and all the sophistry in the world cannot free them from the degradation and dishonour of having done so. But we must remember that Europe in that day, greatly as it had advanced in civilisation, was still far behind the point it has since reached, and that if the French are to be censured for what they did in Egypt it is not because we in England were incapable of evil; nay, what, after all, was the torture inflicted upon the Sheikh el

Sadat to that inflicted by the law of England on a mere boy sentenced to be flogged once a fortnight for two years? or to the flogging of a seaman "round the fleet" that was so often carried out long after?

For sheer brutality and gross wanton inhumanity the world has scarcely any record that can approach that of the "Holy Office," but the records of England's prisons are not far behind, and leave us no room for anything but shame and humility on the score of our humanity in the past. It is not therefore to picture the French as monsters of iniquity that I have spoken of this matter, but as the natural reply of the Egyptian when he is accused, as he so often is, of ingratitude and want of appreciation of the blessings that we good, kind-hearted Europeans have so generously bestowed upon him. To the European critic of Egypt and its affairs the benefits conferred upon the country and its people by the introduction of European civilisation are so great and so many as to overshadow and hide all else.

Unfortunately it is not so to the Egyptian. He knows only too well that there has been a reverse side to the picture that the European draws. The evils of which I have been speaking have long since passed away, but they have left a trail of bitter feeling that still survives. Some of the most prominent of the Egyptian citizens of Cairo today, (as at time of first publication), are the direct descendants of the men who suffered so severely under the French. Would it be human in them to forget that to the present day they are sufferers from the ills their immediate ancestors had to bear? And yet these men, true to the traditions of their families, are today as they were in the time of the French, the men most ready to give a cordial welcome to all real progress—men who, though they cannot forget the past, are content to bury its bitterness and who fully recognise that the Europe of today is not altogether the same thing as the Europe of a century ago.

Yet one word more is necessary on this subject. Whatever truth there was in the French excuse that they were but "doing in the East what the Easterns did," this was not true of the Egyptians. All historians agree in one thing—that from the earliest days down to the French occupation (which, as we have seen, was the introduction of an era of "liberty, equality, and fraternity") the Egyptian people had always been the downtrodden slaves of the long string of foreign rulers who had exploited them in the most merciless manner. Yet in these same histories we find the people spoken of as if they had been the rulers, and all the vices and sins of the Mamaluks, their followers and their servants the Copts, are put down with a most generous impartiality to the unhappy people who had to bear the bitter burthen these sins and vices cast upon them. Tyranny, torture, bribery, corruption were rife in the country, therefore the Egyptians were tyrannical, corrupt, and so on.

And the same writers, with a calm indifference to the claims of logic and common sense not altogether peculiar to them, tell us that the people were slothful, lacking in energy, content to live from hand to mouth, servile and, to cap the pyramid of their faults and follies, fatalists! How is it that these brilliant historians are unable to see that the centre and controlling feature of all the history of the country has been the utter irreconcilability of the characters of the ruled and their rulers? This was so in the days of the Ptolemies and of the *caliphs* as in the days of the Mamaluks and of the French.

Crushing as was the indemnity imposed by the French upon the miserable citizens of Cairo, it was not in the eyes of the Egyptians the worst of the evils from which they had to suffer. We have seen that in their day of trouble the Christians, if they had found assailants among the Moslems, had also found very vigorous protectors. Now that the Christians had an opportunity of showing their gratitude they hastened to do so. The French, with a paltry spite that admits no excuse, forbade the Moslems to ride, commanded them, under pain of the bastinado, to stand up whenever a Frenchman passed, and in other ways sought to humiliate them as much as possible, not the least being the permission they tacitly, if not directly, accorded the native Christians to insult, abuse, and ill-treat the Moslems.

And all this was done to "Our people" in virtue of the "Amnesty" that had been granted, not in the fiery heat of open hostility or wrath, or to crush opposition, but with deliberate vindictiveness when all excuse for such brutality had ceased. And the native Christians, following the good example set them and in gratitude for the protection they had received from Moslem defenders, availed themselves to the utmost of the privilege accorded them.

It has been said that this was but a recoil upon the Moslems of ill-treatment they had in times past inflicted upon the Christians. No falser excuse could be offered. It is true that, as I have before admitted, the lower classes of the Moslems had constantly insulted and ill-used the Christians, and under some of the *sultans* these had been subjected to degrading and vexatious tyrannies; but, as we have seen, the better class of the people and the Moslem rulers in general always afforded them the full and ample protection to which they were entitled in accordance with Moslem law and religion, even when the granting of that protection necessitated the shedding of Moslem blood.

Never once in the history of the country had the Christians been without some of the Moslems for their protectors, and never once had the Moslems, in cool blood or with deliberate malice, persecuted them as native and European Christians now persecuted the Moslems. In moments of wrath and of political excitement Christians had been massacred and their houses pillaged, the lower classes were habitually offensive to them, they had been subjected to humiliating conditions and restrictions by some of the rulers of the land as they had been petted and pampered by others, but with all this they had always been not worse but better off than the bulk of the Moslems. Nor must it be forgotten that it was not as Christians, but as the servants of the government, that the Christians were hated by the people. Bigots and fanatics have existed, such as Nasooh Pacha, but they were and are regarded by all true Moslems as little better than heretics and infidels. Nowhere throughout Islam are Christians hated as Christians, or for the sake of their religion, but for their actions towards and treatment of Moslems.

No better evidence of the true relations between the two peoples or of their conduct to each other can be asked for than that afforded by Gabarty's history, with its perfect freedom from bigotry and fanaticism. So far from exonerating or condoning the faults of the Moslems, he speaks of and condemns these more frequently and more freely than those of the Christians, and the fact that he does so is the more noticeable, and by far the more significant, that he was writing, not for Christian or European readers, but solely for his countrymen and coreligionists. Nor can we forget in weighing its value that, plain-spoken as it is on the faults and failings of the Moslems, it is the most popular history written in their language. If the Moslems of Egypt were the bitter fanatics they are so commonly accused of being this could not be so.

But that the Moslems never did oppress the Christians is proved by the simple historical fact, attested by all the Christian historians of the country, that, from the first introduction of Islam into the country down to the present day, the Moslem Egyptians have never had the power or means of oppressing or tyrannising over the Christians or anyone else. Not only so, but they have never had the means or the power to protect themselves from the tyranny and oppression of the Christians. Under the *caliphs* and their successors the Mamaluks whatever there was of tyranny and oppression fell with fullest weight upon the Moslems. Their grievances were real enough, and not, as were those of the Christians, little more than sentimental; the *kurbag*, the *corvée*, extortion and injustice of every kind, were the evils from which the Moslems had to suffer, while for the most part the Christians escaped these and had as their chief grievances the facts that they were treated socially as an inferior race, were not allowed to ride horses, or to hold land, and had to wear a distinctive dress. And as a set-off to these grievances they had no small share in the golden harvest extorted by cruelty and torture from the Moslems. What wonder if the Moslems felt bitterly against them, or that their bitterness was increased by their impotency to protect themselves. And yet, save for such wild outbursts as that incited by Nasooh Pacha, they were content to leave the Christians alone.

And when we recall the relative position of the Christians and the Moslem people in the country we cannot be surprised that the bitterness I have spoken of should develop into hatred. So far as the people were concerned, it was the Christians, and the Christians alone, who were mainly responsible for their sufferings. It was the Christians who were the real oppressors of the people. They constituted the one class in the country which, if it had willed to do so, could have softened the endless sufferings of the people—the one class that, without a complete change in the government, could have benefited them. But far from benefiting they were the one and only class that in season and out of season never ceased to pursue the miserable people day or night, grinding them in the dust from pure malicious hatred.

It was they who carried on the atrocious tyranny that wrecked the commerce of the country and well-nigh desolated the land, for it was they who fixed and they who collected the assessments that crushed and starved the peasantry. They might, with little loss to themselves, have vastly bettered the condition of the people, but far from doing so they pushed their power for evil to the utmost. That is why the Moslems hated them. Ruthless, savage as were the Mamaluks, they were always under some restraint. As a mere matter of policy they could not wholly resist the intercessions of the *ulema*, and so it was to their Coptic and other Christian clerks that the *beys* turned for advice and counsel as to how much and how the people could be forced to pay.

The *beys* thought nothing of annihilating a village that would not or could not pay the sum demanded of it, but it was the Christian clerks of the *beys* who fixed the amount to be paid and who persuaded the *beys* that it was unwillingness and not inability that kept the people from paying. These are facts that cannot be denied or disputed. They are practically admitted by all historians, none of these failing to point out that the administrative branch of the government has always been in the hands of the Christians, though none of them seem to have ever cared to recognise the logical and inevitable consequence of this fact.

It was not in the power of the Christians to have wholly averted the evils from which the people had to suffer, but they might have done much that would have vastly mitigated not only the outrageous extortion practised but also the cruelty and brutality with which it was enforced. It was, then, not as Christians but as their heartless oppressors that the Moslems hated the Christians, and the sole excuse that these could offer for their wanton inhumanity was the contempt and social ill-treatment they received, not from the people but from the men they served.

And as it was with the Christians of the country so it was with the French—whatever of hatred the people had for them was due not to religious fanaticism or bigotry but to the oppression they inflicted upon the people.

I have dwelt upon this point at the greater length that I am convinced of the importance of the European critics of Egypt and the Egyptians learning to look at this question from the true point of view. At the present day it is the commonly asserted belief of almost all the Europeans in the country that the Egyptians are a bigoted and fanatical race. I deny it entirely. I have travelled and lived among Moslems in more lands than one, among Kurds and Afghans, Indians and others, and I have never met a Moslem people not only so free from fanaticism but so lax, from the Moslem point of view, as the Egyptians.

Nor must the reader forget two points that tend to show that the bitterness of the people towards the Christians was the result of political and not of religious animosity. These facts are that Moslems of whose orthodoxy there was no doubt were during the revolt and during the siege assaulted, ill-treated, and in more than one case killed, by the mob on the accusation of befriending or simply of being in sympathy with the French. The Sheikh El Sadat was one of those who had to suffer in this way, and almost all of the *sheikhs* who had gone as a deputation to treat for peace during the siege.

So, on the other hand, the Jews, who have always refrained from interfering in politics, and who have ever been studiously careful to avoid taking sides with any party or sect in the country, although they are the subject of far stronger personal and religious dislike than are the Christians, were never the object of direct attack from the people, though they, like the Moslems, on many occasions suffered when the mob broke out against the Christians.

In the time of the French occupation the Harat el Yahoud, or Jews' Quarter, was situated, as it still is, off the Mousky, then the principal residence of the Franks and Christians, yet in the list that Gabarty gives of the quarters of the town that had been raided by the mob this is not included. All through the troubled days of the French occupation the Jews had to bear their share of the ills that fell upon all; but the people bore them no special hatred, had no special grievance against them, did not look upon them as their personal enemies, and thus they escaped the direct attacks that were made upon the Christians.

The hatred, then, with which the Egyptians had learned to regard the French was not the hatred of fanaticism and had but little reference to the question of religion. Had the French understood the people and been willing and able to rule them with due regard for their prejudices and desires, there was no reason why they should not have gained the goodwill, and with certain limitations, the loyalty of the people. It was not only possible for the French to have done this, but it would have been easier for them to do so than to follow the mad course they chose to adopt. The fact of the French being Christians, for as such the Egyptians regarded them, would have had but small weight if they had conceded to Moslem sentiment its reasonable demands. T

o the Egyptian mind the Mamaluks were not much better Moslems than the French might easily have been. This the French could not see, and not being able to see it, or to understand the people, they could find no other way to rule them but that which the Mamaluks had adopted—force. And it was with them as with every government that has ever existed or ever can exist, the admission that it is compelled to use force to rule any people whatever is a confession that the task of rightly ruling that people is beyond their strength, that it is one for which they are unfitted and one in which they never can succeed. It is a law of nature in the moral as in the physical world and one from which there is no escape—that no force can operate without creating resistance to its own action, and the greater the force the greater the resistance. A given force may for a time appear to crush all opposition, but if it could do so in reality it would be but to find itself exhausted and effete.

Unable to understand either the people of Egypt or their history, the French could not see that while for centuries the rule of the country had been founded upon force, it had been maintained not by force but by the pliancy of its rulers. No one knew this better than the Mamaluk chiefs. These cared nothing for the people or their desires, and they never hesitated to drive them to the uttermost, but they knew equally well that there was a limit and, though they but yielded to conquer, they yielded when that limit was reached. Nor did they, like the French, waste their force in unprofitable directions or in exciting needless opposition, but devoted it wholly and solely to the attainment of their one great object—the procuring of the funds they needed.

In the East the shepherd goes before his flock; whither he leads they follow, and his dogs serve only to bring up the stragglers or hasten the steps of the laggards. It is much the same with the people. *Caliphs, sultans, beys,* and French may seem to be driving them, but in reality they are not being driven but led, led by perhaps unseen and unknown shepherds that are yet more potent for good or evil than any ruler that ever sat on an Eastern throne. Europeans cannot see this, yet every Eastern who has given the subject a moment's thought knows that it is so. As often as not the real leader and ruler of the people is himself unconscious of his power or position. It was so in the days before the revolt of Cairo.

An open avowed leader the people would most probably have distrusted, but the almost silent man who said but little, who assumed no authority but rightly gauged the feelings stirring around him and knew how, by simple words, to influence the current of those feelings, could sway the people as he willed. The demagogue who cries aloud in the market-places, bidding men accept him as their guide and friend, obtains but a poor following. He may stir up latent feeling to action, but he cannot direct either the feeling or the action. So far as he can rightly interpret the feeling he may pose as the spokesman and leader of a party, but true leader he never is.

Mahdis are forever arising to preach, like Peter the Hermit, the glory and duty of a "Holy War," but among the people of the East they gain but poor success. The negro races flock to the standards of these men and have died in thousands for their sake, but the Eastern asks for a miracle before he will be convinced, and, holding aloof from the would-be guide, follows all unknowingly some other.

If the reader has followed me so far he will now have pretty clearly grasped the truth that the rule of the French in Egypt had proved an utter failure, and to some extent he will have seen why this was so. That failure was brought about by not one but many causes. Of these, besides those that I have already dealt with, there is one that I may speak of here.

I have shown in a previous chapter how, although the teachings of the Christian and Mahomedan religions are almost identical as to the duty of obedience to those in authority, the varying circumstances affecting the peoples of England and those of the East lead these to interpret and apply those teachings very differently. It is so with other matters. Christianity and Islam are at one in ranking Justice and Mercy as the greatest of the virtues. "*The Lord thy God*" is "*a just God*," but also "*a merciful God*" is the teaching of the *Koran* as well as of the Bible. It is the belief of the Moslem as well as of the Christian. But the European conception of justice is to the Moslem, and indeed to all Easterns, hopelessly imperfect, so imperfect that in their eyes it becomes injustice.

One law for all, for high and low, rich and poor. That is the ideal of civilised Europe—an ideal that never has been and in all probability never will be accepted in the East. The man of high position who commits an offence should, says the West, be punished in the same way and in the same degree as an humbler man would be for the same offence. That, says the East, is just in theory but impossible in practice. And the East is right. In no conceivable case is it possible to accord to two men an exactly equal amount of punishment. Whether it be a sixpenny fine or the death penalty, every penalty inflicted affects the person upon whom it is inflicted precisely in proportion to facts and circumstances that it is not possible should be known to or weighed by his judge. That this is so is admitted by all, but in England and other countries men are content with an attempt at "justice" that almost wholly ignores this fact. Not so the Easterns. That one of the *ulema*, a *pacha* or any other person of position should be punished by a penalty such as might be inflicted upon any ordinary citizen is to the Eastern mind not justice but gross injustice.

But the difference in the Englishman's conception of justice and that of the Eastern lies even deeper than this. To the English mind the idea of justice is mainly associated with the administration of punishment to the guilty and with abstention from injustice in dealing with others. The Eastern, until he has acquired that tinge of European thought and sentiment that unconsciously yet constantly causes him to mislead Europeans as to what is and what is not Eastern thought on such subjects, but rarely connects the idea of punishment with that of justice. To him punishment is not the administration of justice but the administration of a deterrent. That as such it may be just or unjust he quite recognises, but the justice or injustice of a punishment is to his mind an incident and not an essential of the punishment, and the justice so often lauded in the East is not the justice of the courts but the personal quality that prevents a man wronging another or leads him when he has acted unjustly to admit his error and seek to remedy it.

And while the two peoples are thus apart in their interpretation of justice, they are still more widely so in the positions they assign to justice and mercy. The European, and perhaps especially the Englishman, places justice first and only allows mercy to come in a long way off. Not so the Eastern. To him mercy is first and justice second. That this should be so is a direct result of the conditions under which the two peoples have lived for many centuries. As all history shows, the races of Europe have always had a genius for and a tendency towards organised government. Whether we peruse the records of liberty-loving England or of thraldom-trodden Spain, of republican France, or of despotic Russia, in every European country we find the people regarding an organised government, a government acting in a prescribed manner upon a prescribed system, as a natural complement of existence as a nation. It is not so in the East.

There the whole bent of opinion tends towards autocratic if not to pure despotic rule. The difference is due to various causes, but possibly to none more than this—that in Europe the community of interests binding individuals together and causing them to recognise each other as members of a group are territorial, limited chiefly and sometimes wholly by geographical boundaries, whereas in the East this community of interest rests almost entirely upon the religious distinctions that divide peoples living in the same countries. In Europe, though there have been religious wars, war has in the main been the result of the rivalries of peoples distinguished from each other by language, habits, and character.

In the East religion has in general been the line of distinction. It has followed from this that in Europe the peoples have been and still are obliged to group themselves as nations, while in the East they group themselves by their religions. The European nation or community is therefore a secular body, and as such seeks a secular government, whereas the Eastern peoples are not nations so much as religious communities. To each an organised government is necessary for self-protection and internal adjustment. This the European is obliged to find in the organisation of a special governing body, while the Easterns find it ready to hand in the organisation of their Churches. Now in the organisation of a nation with regard to its internal affairs, justice is almost of necessity placed before mercy, whereas in that of a religion, mercy is exalted above justice.

Hence a people like the English learn to look upon justice, or whatever near approach to it can be attained, as the greatest good to be sought for from their rulers and in their efforts to attain this end, like the political economists of whom Ruskin complained, forget the human equation, and that justice, however finely balanced by tale and weight of legal prescription, can never be more nor less than a failure, if it be not dominated by mercy. In Europe peoples have again and again revolted against the tyrants that have oppressed them that they might thereby secure justice and its complement liberty, and they could do this because there was no higher or conflicting interest to hold them back; but it has not been so in the East.

There all the organisation that the peoples have needed for the administration of their internal affairs has always been found in the organisation of their religion, and whether the tyranny and oppression from which they have suffered from times immemorial afflicted them through the hands and acts of their co-religionists or from those of other and rival religions, the interests of their religion, and therefore of their fellows, demanded submission to such ills rather than a resistance that could not fail to injure that which they deemed the higher and better cause. And in the sufferings they were thus called upon to bear they naturally turned to their religion for consolation, and found it in their belief in the ineffable mercy of the Deity, and thus learning to look upon mercy as the highest attribute of God inevitably rank it as the noblest virtue in man.

And to the Moslem the appreciation of mercy he thus acquires is enforced by the teaching of the *Koran*. The law of retaliation, an eye for an eye, is ordained to Moslems, but with the promise that to him who exacts less his forbearance shall be accounted as a charity and as such shall gain him a rich reward. To bridle one's anger, to forgive men and to intercede "with a good intercession"—these are virtues that are endlessly praised and commended in *The Book of God*.

What a poor substitute for these is the "even-handed justice" that is the boast of our vaunted civilisation!

Is it necessary for me to say now that the price the French asked the people of Cairo to pay for the peace that had been accorded them, was to them a violation of all justice? Or need I point out at length that this incompatibility of ideals on the subjects of justice and mercy was one of the principal causes of the failure of the French to realise the anticipations with which they had entered the country, as it is still one of the causes that hold the East and West apart, and forms a never-resting cause of misunderstanding between all Orientals and Europeans.

Unfortunately in this, as in other matters, the Oriental is too prone to keep his ideals as a standard whereby to judge the merits and failings of others, rather than as a guide for his own actions. It is one of the greatest of the Englishman's merits that he does not do this. He strives as best he may to realise his ideals, and in this it would be well indeed for the Egyptian to imitate him. With both people, as indeed with all others if we would judge them justly, we must, however, take account first of their ideals and next of the sincerity and earnestness with which they seek to bring these into practice.

CHAPTER 15

An Ungrateful People

Boulac had fallen on the 14th of April, 1800. Exactly two months later, on the 14th of June, General Kleber was assassinated. He was taking a morning walk in the garden of General Dugua's house, when a young man, a Syrian, approached him as if to offer a petition, and before the unfortunate general could detect his purpose, struck him several blows in the breast with a dagger. The assassin was arrested soon after, and made a confession. Of his guilt there could be no doubt, but his confession being made under torture was of course perfectly worthless. In it he stated that he had been employed to commit the infamous deed by a high officer of the Turkish Army that Kleber had defeated at Materiah. That he was a Syrian, and that he had only been in Egypt for a few weeks, were facts that were easily established. The French believed, however, that he was encouraged if not instigated by Egyptians, and although there was absolutely nothing to suggest that this was the case, except perhaps their keen sense of the hatred with which they were regarded, they determined to discover all that could be discovered of the origin of the crime.

The wretched prisoner was therefore handed over to the care of the chief of the police, a Greek of infamous character, a notorious evil-liver, detested and abhorred by all for his wanton cruelties, abominable vices, and utter depravity. Selected for the post he held as one whose unbridled and unconcealed hatred for the people of the country was a guarantee of his fidelity to the French, his selection is an all too eloquent testimony as to the real nature of the relations between the French and the Egyptians. No man viler, more depraved, or more despicable, could have been placed in a position such as that accorded to this villain—a position that practically placed him above and beyond all law and all restraint, and gave free scope to his inhumanity, his outrageous vices, and devilish passions.

Like Oates, he delighted to seduce and betray his fellow-men; like Jeffreys, he rejoiced when sending them to prison, torture, or death; like the caitiff James, he revelled in witnessing their anguish and agonies. To this wretch Kleber's assassin was handed over, and by him almost all that could be done by torture or otherwise to induce the criminal to denounce others as his accomplices or abettors was tried. At length, when all other means had failed to accomplish the end at which he aimed, the wretch persuaded his miserable victim, by a promise of free pardon to himself, to give the names of some *sheikhs* of the Azhar to whom, as he admitted, he had made known the purport of his visit to Cairo.

One of these *sheikhs*, it was found, had already left the country, but the others were at once arrested. These admitted that they had been spoken to on the subject by the prisoner, but asserted, and as it would appear truly, that they had endeavoured to dissuade him from the commission of the crime, and, on finding that he persisted in his intention, had kept aloof from him; but while granting the full value of the plea the *sheikhs* thus offered, it must be admitted that the French were justified, by all known law and custom, in sentencing them to death, as, had they denounced the Syrian's intention, there is no doubt but that his crime would have been effectually prevented.

The sentence passed upon the assassin does not admit of equal justification. Kleber, whatever his faults or errors as an administrator, or however harsh and faithless his treatment of the Egyptians had been, was a brave and gallant gentleman, a man of whom his countrymen were and are justly proud, and one who had endeared himself to all under his command, while in the position in which they then were the whole body of the French looked up to him as the only one from whom they could seek or obtain the leadership so essential to their almost desperate case. But with the fullest sympathy for the bitterness of spirit that must at the moment have oppressed the French, it is impossible to condone the sanction they accorded to the base treachery of their minion, the chief of the police, by whom the pardon he had promised the assassin, as the price to be paid him for giving up the names of the *sheikhs*, was withdrawn immediately the names had been given, and without the slightest pretext being offered for this vile breach of faith.

Nor can the sentence passed be regarded as otherwise than a brutal one, though it was not indeed more so than others that have been passed by nations and peoples claiming to represent the most advanced civilisation. It was that the prisoner's right hand should be cut off, that he should witness the execution of the *sheikhs*, and that he should himself be impaled alive.

The execution of the condemned men was fixed to take place immediately after the funeral of the general, and it was wholly in vain that some of the *sheikhs* and notables pleaded for a mitigation of the penalty. On the appointed day the prisoners were marched out to a rising ground on the route the general's funeral was to follow, and posted there, at the spot selected for the execution, they were compelled to view the mournful procession that, with all the pomp of a State ceremony, accompanied the general's remains to the temporary burial-ground in which they were to be laid. There, on the completion of the funeral rites, the sentences on the condemned men were carried out, and the *sheikhs* having been beheaded the wretched assassin was impaled alive and left to linger in the most horrible anguish for over four hours.

A punishment such as this was not then, nor ever can be, other than purely and simply an act of vengeance. In the East especially it is but a perversion of terms to pretend that such penalties can be justified as deterrents. History proves conclusively that they have no such effect, except perhaps for the moment, but that they have the effect of hardening and brutalising the hearts of those they are supposed to terrify is certain. In the present case there was not even the slightest ground of excuse. The criminal was a foreigner, and it had been clearly proved at his trial that his crime had met with no encouragement or sympathy from the people of the country. The whole conduct of the people from the first arrival of the French had been sufficient to show that there was absolutely no reason to suspect them of any desire to repeat, in any form, the crime that this foreigner had committed.

Three times "peace" had been declared in Cairo by the French, and three times the people—though on two occasions most unwillingly accepting the peace—had kept it loyally and with the most perfect and submissive good faith. In the revolt and the siege they had shown with what pleasure they could set themselves to the task of slaying the French, but peace once declared all ranks and grades of Frenchmen went about in perfect safety. The French complained that the people were ungrateful; but does it not seem that the people might have retorted that the French were infinitely more so?

There remains but little to be said of the French occupation. After the death of Kleber the command of the army devolved upon General Menou.

As he had for some time professed himself a convert to Islam, and had married a woman of the country, it might have been thought that the change would have tended to promote better feelings between the two peoples. It proved otherwise. None of the Egyptians believed in the sincerity of the general's conversion, and it had therefore no other effect than to discredit the professions of sympathy for Islamic ideas that other Frenchmen made, and perhaps to raise hopes that were not to be fulfilled.

As a measure tending to conciliate French feeling, the *ulema* had asked for and obtained permission to close the Azhar mosque, which, from its great extent and the straggling, irregular arrangement of its courts and their surrounding buildings, was of all others the place most capable of affording shelter to strangers visiting the town with evil intent. But the French were quite unable to appreciate the true meaning of this action, and, actuated by a vindictive spirit most unworthy of a civilised people, sought further vengeance for the crime of a foreigner upon the unhappy Egyptians. A heavy "contribution" was therefore exacted, and European and native Christians vied with each other in heaping insult and contumely upon the Moslems. Some steps were indeed taken by Menou that seem to have been intended to favour the Moslems and gain their support.

Thus the *dewan* was reorganised, and, for the first time under the French, was composed exclusively of Mahomedans, one French official only being appointed to assist at its meetings. In the government service also Copts were largely replaced by Mahomedans—a step that exceedingly embittered the Copts—and the French were subjected to the taxes from which they had theretofore been free—a measure that excited their indignation. With scarcely an exception, the French were heartily sick of the country. All the enthusiasm by which they had at first been stimulated had vanished. They had arrived in Egypt, looking for a sojourn that should be a triumphal progress towards the attainment of great ideals and vast projects.

It was to be the first step, as they had hoped, towards making France the Mistress of the World, but, save for the first victory over the Mamaluks, the story of their stay in the land was little else but one of disappointments, losses and vexations; for the suppression of the revolt, the routing of the Turkish Army, and the retaking of Cairo were not events upon which they could look with other than bitter feelings, since, although victories, all the circumstances surrounding them tarnished the little glory they might have possessed under happier conditions. But General Menou was not so weary or so hopeless as his countrymen; he still thought it possible to colonise the country and to establish French influence upon a safe basis.

It had been the blunder, or rather the weakness, of Bonaparte and Kleber, that they had not realised the truth Burke taught, that "The temper of the people amongst whom he presides ought to be the first study of a statesman." Bonaparte had thought to win his way by wheedling, and, failing to do so, had turned to force. Kleber had had no other conception than that of "the iron hand," as we nowadays term it, and had not the tact to clothe it with the pretence of a glove. Menou seems to have sought to play the part of the old man in the fable, and try to please everybody, with the inevitable result of pleasing none.

On the one hand, as we have just seen, he favoured the Moslems in some few respects, on the other he offended their keenest prejudices by allowing wine to be sold and drunk openly in the streets, while, encouraged by the protection granted them by the French, the lowest classes of the Christians and Mahomedans gave themselves up to an open practice of vice and immorality that had never before been permitted. This alone was a wanton outrage upon the sentiments of the whole of the respectable population, Christian as well as Mahomedan, that was sufficient to make the French hated and detested by all but the most debased—a class which in Egypt, even today, after a century of the nourishing protection of European civilisation, is infinitely smaller in proportion to the population than in any other country, except a few like Persia, that are almost entirely outside of or beyond that protection.

Not that the French in Egypt by any means laid themselves open to a charge of profligacy. There seems no reason to believe that they did anything of the kind, but that which to them was entirely unobjectionable was to the Easterns, among whom they were dwelling, utterly abominable. Thus the drinking of wine in public, and the free intercourse of the two sexes in public places, however innocent to the French, were to the Egyptians something more than simply distasteful; and that they should be so is a matter not only of custom and habit, but one of climatic and other conditions which Europeans ignore. To the Moslem peoples these things are subject to the further objection that they are opposed to the teaching of their religion.

At length the day came for the French to go. The English and the

Turks had brought their combined forces to bear, and not only was an English fleet once more off Alexandria, but Colonel Baird, with a strong force of *sepoy* soldiers from India, had arrived by the Red Sea.

For the French to have attempted to hold out against the enemy that was now at their door would have been an act of madness, but it was at least possible for them to ask and to obtain honourable terms; and these having been granted, the evacuation of the country was agreed upon, and the French, rejoiced at the prospect of once more returning to their beloved native land, for the second time during their stay prepared to quit a country to which so many bitter memories were attached. In June, 1801, just a year after the death of Kleber, the French garrison of Cairo capitulated, but Menou held out for some time longer, and only resigned himself to the inevitable on the 30th of August, and on the 18th of September sailed for Europe.

Thus ingloriously ended the great dream of a French Empire in the East. At Cairo nothing could exceed the joy of the people as they at last saw the now utterly hated and detested foreigners leaving. In their case it was eminently true that "the evil that men do lives after them." They had sown the seeds of a bitterness of feeling towards all Europeans, and of a mistrust of European civilisation, that still bear fruit and still retard the advancement of the country. It was the French occupation that proved the greatest difficulty and stumbling-block in the way of the English occupation, and for such a long time rendered the task that the English administrators had undertaken seem almost a forlorn hope. Every promise and pledge offered by the English was weighed in the scale of those made by Bonaparte and his successors.

Every profession of respect for the institutions and religion of the country was interpreted by the recollection of the French cavalry stabled in the Azhar, and the tyrannies, vexations, and outrages upon their most cherished prejudices that the people had sustained under the French. It has been the custom to trace to the French occupation whatever advance the country has since made. In two ways only had it any lasting beneficial effect—it brought to the attention of the few men like Gabarty a keen sense of the great advantages of an orderly government, and a warm appreciation of the advance that science and learning had made in Europe, and it opened the way for the man who was to be the real founder and maker of the Egypt of today.

These were the only two benefits that the French left behind them, and the greatest of these was quite unintentional and unforeseen. As to all else, the occupation left nothing but evil memories and evil influences behind it. It had lowered the moral standard of the lowest classes, had taught these to look upon vice and immorality from a new and more debasing point of view, and had almost wholly destroyed the controlling influence the *ulema* and better classes had theretofore exercised upon them. European historians have never seen that this is so—that they should fail to see it is not surprising, since even the Europeans living in the country are incapable of perceiving it. The European's standard of morality is so different to that of the Eastern, and he is so fanatically attached to his own ideas that he cannot understand any one rejecting these, except from sheer perversity. For thousands of years the Egyptians have been accustomed to bathe freely in the Nile, today they are debarred at Cairo and elsewhere, lest the sight of a nude figure should shock some sensitively minded European who happens to look up from his, or her, perusal of the latest London society scandal. It is so much easier to see the mote than the beam!

The modern Englishman will scarcely admit that his ancestors who, in the time of Shakespeare and long after, were accustomed to call a spade a spade, and never blushed to crack a plain-spoken jest, had in truth a moral standard higher than his own, and that the man who keeps these things for his intimate friends and his hours of abandon is less healthy in mind and morals than the man who thinks no shame to speak them openly. The difference between the two types is the difference that prevails between the European and the Oriental standard of decency. Hence today, as in the time of the French occupation, the verdict that either of the peoples would pass upon the decency and morality of the other, would be utter condemnation.

But this fact remains—that throughout the whole of Islam openly practised vice and immorality exist only under the actively exercised protection of the Christian Powers. Not only so, but if the traveller wishes to gauge with infallible accuracy the extent of the influence exercised by the Christian Powers in any Mahomedan country, he can do so by simply ascertaining the extent of the open vice and immorality that is permitted. This is the true hall-mark of European civilisation in Moslem lands.

But among the Frenchmen with the expedition there were, as there always are when a number of Frenchmen are brought together, men of high ideals, men whom to know is to esteem. From their altogether too restricted and hampered intercourse with such, the men of kindred type among the *ulema* and notables learned to appreciate, to some extent, the better side of European civilisation. They saw clearly, too, that there was nothing in the civilisation that such men represent-ed that could be held as inimical to Islam or contrary to its teaching. To the present day the conviction they thus acquired is bearing good fruit. Prior to the French occupation, thanks to the utter isolation of the country, it was the common and universal belief that everything connected with the social and moral condition of Europeans was in its nature essentially anti-Islamic and accursed.

Precisely the same idea still widely prevails in Persia and other parts of the Mahomedan East today, as well as throughout the whole of the North of Africa. But the truly honest man, honest in spirit as well as deed, recognises his fellow of whatever race, religion, or speech he may be. Gabarty and his peers in Cairo were no exception to the rule, and could discern with infallible accuracy the men who really desired to benefit the country and the people. For such they had unbounded goodwill and respect, and through their intercourse with these they acquired some knowledge of the latent possibilities of that civilisation of which the expedition, as a whole, was such a poor exponent.

It was in this way that the arrival of the French in Egypt was, as I have termed it, "The dawn of the new period," but I have used the word "dawn" as the only one the language gives me, though it does not rightly express the meaning I wish to convey, for this dawn of the new period was not the "bright, rosy dawn of day," but the faint, dimly discernible dawn to which the Arabs give the name of "*el Fujr.*" The true dawn was to come later, and its herald was to be not a French-man, nor a man of learning or culture, but a Moslem, an illiterate and wholly self-made man.

I have had to say some hard things of the French, but before pass-ing on to consider the events that followed their departure I must pause to say that I would not have the reader suppose that in speaking of the occupation, I have myself forgotten the necessity of remember-ing time and place I pointed out to others in an earlier chapter. In this, as in other things, the reader must remember that I am in this book endeavouring to present to him the story of the development of modern Egypt as it presents itself to one who knows the Egyptians of today, and who, from his religious and other sympathies with them, can understand how the events of which he speaks has affected them in the past and does so in the present.

There is no charge more constantly or more unjustly brought against the Egyptian than that he is ungrateful for the benefits and blessings that European Governments and peoples have conferred upon him. The charge, I repeat, is absolutely unjust, and could never be made were it not for the failure of those who make it to recognise two of the most important factors in the evidence they ought to weigh before attempting any judgment upon the question. These factors are—first, that the Egyptians and their rulers were never one and the same people, and secondly, that to a large extent the very things for which their gratitude is asked are frequently those that most grate upon their feelings and susceptibilities.

I have pointed out these facts before, but they are so constantly and so widely ignored that I desire to impress them upon the reader's attention in the hope that he, at least, will in future bear them in mind whenever he is called upon or tempted to criticise the Egyptians. It has, therefore, been from no wish to say unkindly things of the French that I have felt bound to speak strongly of the darker side of the French occupation. This should indeed be clear from the references I have made to the conditions prevailing in England at that time. I no more think that the French in Egypt were actuated by any evil or ignoble intentions than that the English Government of that day did not believe itself the most perfect conceivable, but the facts of history show that both were, in blundering ignorance, pursuing their way by means and methods that truth, justice, and equity must condemn.

If, then, any French reader should feel aggrieved by what I have said of the occupation, him console himself with my assurance that, if I had been writing of the English Government of that day and its conception of justice, I should have had to denounce it as one of the most brutal and brutalising ever known, and infinitely worse than any that Egypt has ever had. Let him who doubts the justice of this judgment turn to the records of the time, or, if he prefers to seek its confirmation in lighter literature, let him take up Dickens's *Barnaby Rudge*.

The failure of the French occupation was due to the fact that it was a military occupation, having for its first and chief aim the acquisition of territory and the extension of empire, and that its leaders were mainly men of the ambitious, unreflecting temperament of the typical soldier, or freebooter, who looks to a victory of arms as the highest and noblest achievement worthy of his efforts. Had it been possible for the French *savants* to have landed in the country alone, and to have pursued their aims in the peaceful way they would have chosen, nothing but good could have come of their presence in the country. But the exigencies of a great military expedition and the selfish aims of its leaders destroyed almost all possibility of the occupation benefiting the country, and, placing endless barriers in the way of those who would and could have influenced the future of the country for the welfare and happiness of the people, baffled all their efforts to do so. It is, and forever must be so.

Civilisation and empire are two different aims; and just as no man can serve two masters, neither can he pursue two aims, least of all two aims that must be in so many points in constant and irreconcilable conflict; not indeed that there is any such incompatibility as to prevent the coexistence of civilisation and empire, but the man or government that seeks to introduce either into a foreign country will forever find that he must sacrifice now one and now the other if he is to attain either. Unhappily, in the French occupation in Egypt it was civilisation that had to give place to empire, and the result, as we have seen, was the utter failure of both. Many thousands of lives had been offered up on the altar of the "Great" Bonaparte's ambition.

When he entered the country the feeling of the people towards Christian Europe was one of disdain, when the last of the expedition had departed it left behind it bitterness and ill-will born of tyranny, broken promises, and outraged prejudices and susceptibilities—a bitterness that all the long years that have since passed have not wholly buried—a bitterness that still exists, and that always will exist, unless and until Christian Europe learns that it has no right to force its ideals upon a Moslem people, and that, however pure and beneficent its intentions may be, so long as it persistently and from day to day insists upon outraging their religious, moral, and social instincts and desires, it has no just ground for accusing them of being an ungrateful people.

* 9 7 8 0 8 5 7 0 6 9 6 7 2 *